T0077849

VOYAGE
TO A STRICKEN LAND
LAND

VOYAGE
TO A STRICKEN
LAND

A Female Correspondent's Account of the Tactical Errors, Wild West Mentality, Brutal Killings, and Widespread Misinformation During the War in Iraq

Sara Daniel

Translated from the French by George Holoch

Arcade Publishing • New York

Copyright © 2006, 2012 by Sara Daniel
English-language translation copyright © 2006, 2012 by Arcade Publishing, Inc.
Foreword copyright © 2012 by Sara Daniel

All Rights Reserved. No part of this book may be reproduced in any manner without the express written consent of the publisher, except in the case of brief excerpts in critical reviews or articles. All inquiries should be addressed to Arcade Publishing, 307 West 36th Street, 11th Floor, New York, NY 10018.

Arcade Publishing books may be purchased in bulk at special discounts for sales promotion, corporate gifts, fund-raising, or educational purposes. Special editions can also be created to specifications. For details, contact the Special Sales Department, Arcade Publishing, 307 West 36th Street, 11th Floor, New York, NY 10018 or arcade@skyhorsepublishing.com.

Arcade Publishing® is a registered trademark of Skyhorse Publishing, Inc.®, a Delaware corporation.

Visit our website at www.arcadepub.com.

10 9 8 7 6 5 4 3 2 1

Library of Congress Cataloging-in-Publication Data is available on file.

ISBN: 978-1-61145-353-9

Printed in the United States of America

Contents

Foreword

In the fall of 2011, Barack Obama declared that the United States would bring all American troops home by the end of the year. I watched the news with a sense of relief. It would be the end of a nearly nine-year military engagement that cost the lives of 4,400 troops and degenerated into a civil war that killed around one hundred thousand Iraqis. As he delivered his statement, I remembered the tears of General Petraeus. In November of 2003, Petraeus was the head of the 101st Airborne Division in Mossul. I met him at a service commemorating the death of seventeen soldiers killed in the collision of two helicopters hit by a rocket-propelled grenade. The general was overwhelmed by sorrow. Though his soldiers probably did not approve of the display, I found it incredibly moving. Here was a man on the brink of climbing to the top of the U.S. military ladder—thereby condoning all of his country's operations—openly and trenchantly lost in his grief. He stood over the crowd like a Cassandra in waiting, a man broken by the death of his soldiers, and perhaps by the specter of their future in Iraq.

During all these years that I have spent covering this unending war, I have certainly been moved to grief. I watched the violence spiral out of control and upon each return trip to this battered nation, realized that many of the people I had met on my previous journeys, of whose hospitality I had partaken, whose stories I had shared, had not survived the escalating conflict. After nearly a decade, what has been the result of Operation Iraqi Freedom? Can Obama rightfully echo his predecessor in saying "mission accomplished?" Even a brief glance over today's Iraq must inspire a resounding "no." The insurgency continues to flare all over the country. The Sunnis, a minority who once had power under Saddam Hussein, now resent the domination of the Shia majority. Mr. Maliki's government arrested more than six hundred people after being warned by the new transition council in

Libya that former members of Saddam Hussein's army were plotting a coup. For the Shia leader, the Libyan tip had given him an excuse to arrest his political opponents and strengthen his own status.

Al Qaeda in Mesopotamia is still in full operation, with new activity almost every week. It has issued warnings about launching attacks to avenge the death of Osama bin Laden. They have not been, unfortunately, empty promises—suicide bombings, IEDs, and indiscriminate killings happen with such frequency in Baghdad, Tikrit, and elsewhere, that these events are no longer front page material. Most damningly, the very thing that the United States wanted to accomplish above all else in Iraq—democracy that would then spread to the rest of the region—has become a hopeful reality everywhere ... except in Iraq. After the beginning of the Arab Spring in February, demonstrations demanding a better government rippled around Iraq too. The Iraqi youth had little faith in this so-called democratic government backed by the United States. The demonstrations, in an echo of their sister protests from around the Middle East, were harshly quashed by the security forces.

Ironically, the U.S. intervention, by bringing the Shia majority to power, reinforced the primacy of American enemies in the region—extremist factions are now out in greater force in Lebanon, Syria, Iran, and Iraq. The occupation and power shift strengthened the antagonism between the Sunnis and the Shias in a relationship that was already famously treacherous, and set the table for ever-escalating violence. It is very difficult to predict the outcome of this new geopolitical situation.

Today, as democratic fever reaches across the Arab world, one cannot stop wondering: Could all of these senseless deaths and the civil war that followed Operation Iraqi Freedom have been prevented? If Saddam had been toppled by his own people, like Qaddafi in Libya or Ben Ali in Tunisia, would things be different? Maybe not. Maybe the bloodshed would have been even greater. We have yet to see how the Arab Spring will play out in the long term. I just returned from the Syria-Lebanon border, where a group of defectors, known as the Free Syrian Army, is fighting guerrilla-style against Assad's regime in a series of skirmishes that could explode into civil war. In the Middle East, every regime change has the potential to become bloody.

The result of the first free election in Tunisia and the success of the Islamic party, Ennhada, is also a matter of concern for those who saluted the democratic uprising. In Tunisia, where, despite the dictatorship, women held near equal status in society, the same women who fought for their country's freedom from tyranny are now concerned for their personal liberty. In Egypt, Christians continue to be harassed and killed in spite of the regime change. And in Libya, the transition council called for an Islamic government that would implement Sharia law across the country, a potentially dangerous prologue to an equally closed regime.

In the end, though, none of these concerns justify an operation carried out in blind vengeance against a country that never contained its stated target. The War in Iraq irrevocably changed the perception and reputation of the United States throughout the world. This war was ultimately a sad episode of American history. We can only hope that the story doesn't get worse, that the withdrawal of the troops doesn't bring more violence and oppression of minority factions. The Middle East is poised on the brink of a sea change. The world has already witnessed both extraordinary courage and extraordinary cruelty in the string of regime changes that have shifted the face of the region. Iraq, now an open wound in the midst of a world in flux, cannot bear any more violence.

—Sara Daniel
2011

Introduction

VERY SIMPLY, it was on the infamous day of September 11, 2001, that I became a war correspondent, much to the dismay of my family, who had long hoped that I would find a path less fraught with danger.

This said, I come from a family of journalists — my father had founded one of the most important and prestigious weekly magazines in France, *Le Nouvel Observateur*, and for many years my mother had been a press photographer — so that I grew up thinking I would never follow any other profession than journalism of one kind or another. When I was a child, I thought that going to work meant going to the newspaper or magazine every day on a normal working schedule, except that on Tuesdays, when you put the issue to bed, you came home at four in the morning. It seemed perfectly normal to me, on those rare occasions when I was allowed to stay up late to watch the magazine being printed, to see in the corridors the pallid, bleary-eyed journalists, whose very lives seemed to be hanging in the balance as they pondered one last time their prose, to make sure it was as good and as tight as they could make it. My childhood was thus steeped in the clatter of the telex machines, the typefaces one saw at the printer's, the weekly editorial meetings, the roar of the presses. It took me a long time to realize that children did not go running off to places where revolutionaries were holding their clandestine meetings or to interview Arab or African chiefs. Nor did I grow up with a blind belief in the importance of the military. On the contrary. My father was a war correspondent covering the colonial wars of the 1960s as North Africa was rising up in rebellion against the French, during which he was shot in the leg. As a result, he went through life with one leg shorter than the other, and I always thought of him as an eternal convalescent.

As I was growing up, the sight of that scar and the endless stories he told and retold impressed me no end: very early on, I realized that war reporters risked their lives, and that real danger, and real wounds, were not just something that happened in the movies.

Growing up, I was also fascinated by the German Occupation and the tales of the people who fought in the Resistance. Although I knew of the period only from books, that strange and difficult time obsessed me. If I had lived then, would I have ratted under torture? Would I have sacrificed myself for my comrades? Vaguely but surely, I felt that I was not meant to be living in this tepid, egotistical period.

As a student, I stamped my feet with impatience as I watched, day by day, the Soviet Union crumble. I remember, too, watching on television a good-looking French journalist in Romania, Patrick Bourrat, who was covering the execution of Ceaucescu. How I wished that I could have been there! And for the first time the idea that I too might some day be a war correspondent crossed my mind: I felt it physically, telling myself I had to make it happen. Some years later, I learned that Patrick had been killed at the start of the Iraq war, struck by an American tank in Kuwait. . . .

My real start as a journalist was in the United States, a country I came to love, where I felt free for the first time, unfettered by the restrictive hierarchies of my native France. My first stint was as an intern at the *Washington Post;* later I was a stringer for a number of French and Canadian media companies, then a full-fledged correspondent for the *Nouvel Observateur.* I wanted to see everything. I crisscrossed the country from one end to the other for more than three years, covering such disparate events as the upheavals and heated debates over affirmative action; the O. J. Simpson trial; the fallout from the Clinton/Monica Lewinsky scandal. Most vividly I remember that day in April 1995 when, stationed in front of the prison in a small town near Oklahoma City, I saw Timothy McVeigh, handcuffed and manacled, pass only a few feet from where I was standing, as the assembled throng booed and hissed. A few days earlier, he had committed the bloodiest terrorist act on American soil that this country had ever known. During that same period I spent a great deal of time studying and writing about right-wing American militias, both in the forests of Arkansas and in their camps in Minnesota. What I recall especially about them was their unmitigated paranoia, based on the Ku Klux Klan. Not only were they obsessed about the American political scene, they were equally fanatic in their hatred of the United Nations, much as another kind of fanatic would be, years later in Iraq. These American "outsiders" reminded me strikingly both of the Islamic fundamentalists I would meet when I began to specialize in the Middle East, and of the extremist Israeli settlers in Gaza who were also awaiting Armageddon.

On September 11, 2001, I was in Jordan doing a story on the Palestinian refugee camps in Amman. That afternoon, I had decided to go visit the ruins of the ancient city of Petra, which had been deserted since the second Intifada. As I left the site after my visit and headed back to Amman, I began to sense that something extraordinary had happened. First of all, there was the man who suddenly emerged from his roadside stall, his voice a mixture of exultation and menace, asking me whether I was pleased or unhappy about what had happened. I had no idea what he was referring to, but when I arrived back in Amman I found the refugee camps exploding with joy. As for the attack itself, I learned the details from the people I had been interviewing, who were using mobile phones to send messages of congratulations to their friends and colleagues throughout the Middle East. As for my interpreter, a young woman whose tight-fitting leotards were not exactly what the Islamic dress code specified, a woman who since my arrival had never missed a chance to praise Osama bin Laden, she was quite simply ecstatic. His daring attacks on the United States homeland, she said, proved once and for all her hero's superiority.

As for me, a Westerner, I had immediately and automatically been classified as an "enemy" by the same people who only hours before had been only too ready and willing to answer my questions thoughtfully and civilly. Even those who were hesitant about expressing their feelings openly, one sensed, were proud and pleased.

That day I felt the die was cast: my responsibility henceforth would be to try to understand and explain this new world schism, this war of civilizations that had already been taking shape for some time, in a sense before my very eyes, for I had spent a good part of my youth in Arab countries. That knowledge, plus my love for the United States, seemed like an order to investigate and report.

On September 11, 2001, my daughter, Hanna, had just turned two, and yet I had no hesitation about leaving, several months later, for Afghanistan. I knew when I left for this divided and isolated country in the throes of a bloody war that I risked being there quite some time. But if my daughter wondered later on how I could have pulled up stakes and left her behind, to expose myself to such dangers, I would tell her, very simply, that I felt it was my bounden duty. (Though that war had just started, it is still not over as I write.) I would tell her, too, that though it was not a French war, it was a war implicating all of us. Which was why, even after two fellow correspondents with whom I was traveling were killed by Taliban bullets on the northern front, I pushed on to Kabul.

And then came the war in Iraq. How could I not be there? A year before the war started, as I describe in these pages, I went there to witness the celebration of Saddam Hussein's birthday. Virtually everyone with whom I talked told me, confidentially, how deeply they hoped for and dreamed of an end to this mad, absurd, bloody dictatorship. And it was my belief, when the war began, that it might well succeed, this dream come true. But visit after visit, experience after experience, error after error, failure after failure, as I covered the war for three years almost uninterruptedly, I saw the fatal spiral of violence spinning out of control. And the plague that the Americans had come to eradicate was daily replaced by another, for which the occupiers were completely unprepared. If I have stayed the course all these years, against the better judgment of not only my friends and family but even the French government, it is because, having come this far, I felt it imperative to face, and hopefully understand, the monster that has been created.

This book begins the day I found myself face to face with the assassins of Nicholas Berg, a twenty-six-year-old businessman and the first American citizen to be kidnapped and decapitated in Iraq. Later I had the dubious honor of meeting the man one sees standing to the right of Abu Musab al-Zarqawi in that all-too-famous photograph seen around the world. Together with the American photographer Stanley Greene, I was the only Western journalist to witness the profanation of the bodies of the four American contractors in Fallujah. Before that I spent a week with the men who carried out the attack on the DHL plane in Baghdad. All during this time I was meeting, interviewing, and befriending many American soldiers, from the lowliest private to colonels and generals. As a result, I have had perhaps more than my share of scoops, though I never thought of them as such: my endless peregrinations throughout the country simply brought me into situations that few others have experienced. And wherever I went, all I was trying to do was understand this new century where such crimes as I have seen are possible. All I can say, of this time and this place, is that it is far too filled with superlatives: too much violence, too much barbarity, too much suffering on both sides. In short, too much war. Sadly, so many of the people I met and talked to are now dead, most of them assassinated.

As for understanding, I still cannot grasp what goes on in a man's head when, in cold blood, he carries out a decapitation, especially when he coolly tells me that he derives "pleasure" from the act. Nor do I comprehend how one can claim to enjoy the prospect of infiltrating a crowd of one's fellow Arabs and blowing them and oneself up. When, too, did these so-called resistance fighters become terrorists? Questions I can raise more easily than answer.

In Iraq, I had the misfortune to descend into hell and the good luck to come out alive. I can say without exaggeration that, though I have returned alive, I have not returned unscathed, for what I have seen and described is deeply embedded in my heart and mind. Whether we like it or not, this new world of terrorists, men possessed, is our world as well.

VOYAGE
TO A STRICKEN
LAND

1

With the Throat Slitters of Fallujah
July 2004

A S A REPORTER COVERING THE WAR IN IRAQ, my goal for the past year had been to enter the insurgents' capital, Fallujah, forbidden to all foreigners — especially journalists. I wished to interview insurgents in an effort to understand and convey to the world at large what made them do what they did. It was an important if self-imposed assignment. After months of trying, using every military and political contact I had, I had all but given up hope. Nonetheless, with the invaluable help of Muhammad, my devoted Iraqi driver cum guide, who had been obliged to give his entire family's whereabouts to the insurgents as guarantee, we finally received an "invitation" to the insurgents' inner sanctum. Fully aware that any mistake on my part would jeopardize Muhammad's wife, children, and family, Muhammad and I left Baghdad for the infamous city with a sense of victory but also with great trepidation.

"I am responsible for the decapitations of the American agent Nicholas Berg, Kim Sun Il, and the Iraqis who spied on us on behalf of the American enemy," said the man before me. He was about thirty, had a short black beard, and was wearing a white tunic. Looking directly at me, he delivered this calmly, without my having asked anything. In fact, he was the one asking the questions: "And what do you think of our combat?"

Suddenly fifteen pairs of eyes focused on me. The elite of the extremist guerrillas of Fallujah were hanging on my every word. I pretended to be absorbed in my glass of tea, examining the tiny grains of sugar mixed at the bottom with the dry black leaves that were swelling with water. My face was impassive, but inside I was swearing at myself. What was I doing in Fallujah, the capital of throat slitters, with the temperature 120° in the shade? I knew I had to keep my composure, and I decided to take a little time before answering the question posed by Omar Hadid.

Was I living through my final minutes? I betrayed no emotion.

I had wanted to come here to this most dangerous town in Iraq. For the last ten days I had been thinking of nothing else and had tormented everyone around me with my obsession.

Once the temperature gets above 120° in Iraq, you move with economy; every step is an enormous effort. But every step I had taken for the ten days while I had been running around Baghdad had pointed to the same goal: to find a way to get to the town where Iraqis themselves no longer went. Yan, my partner and the father of my daughter, tired of spending summers apart, had surprised me by buying a ticket to spend a few days with me in Baghdad. He was the only "tourist" in a city where every foreigner is involved in the war in some capacity. He stood out. Everyone must have thought he was a spy. I found his gesture a moving sign of love, and was touched that he wanted to understand and see for himself how I worked and what I did during the long weeks when I was not with him and Hanna. In Baghdad, he was able to come along with me to meet the sheikhs and to the most clandestine guerrilla hideouts. My Fallujah obsession was contagious, and soon Yan shared my fixation on how to get to the forbidden town.

And then, one morning when I no longer expected it, the invitation I had been working so hard for finally arrived. Omar Hadid, al-Zarqawi's right-hand man in Iraq, head of the Fallujah mujahideen council, had agreed to meet me the next day in Fallujah. I was not yet aware of the close connection between the military leader Hadid and the Jordanian terrorist who had declared his allegiance to Osama bin Laden. I only knew that Hadid was an "eminent" member of the resistance to the occupation and that his headquarters were in the accursed city of Fallujah, capital of the anti-American insurrection, capital of Iraq's very own Bermuda Triangle.

My Iraqi friends hated all the media hype about this little town, a way station on the road to Jordan. "It's a provincial town swarming with smugglers," they kept telling me, when I mentioned I had seen it gradually turn into the epicenter of the jihad against the West. Personally, I had nothing but unpleasant memories of the place. My first time in Fallujah, a year before, I had been chased out of town at gunpoint, and the last time, the American photographer Stanley Greene and I, the only Westerners there that day, found ourselves witnessing with horror the desecration of the bodies of the four American contractors. That nightmare vision still haunts me today.

Since the Americans had laid siege to Fallujah in April 2004, no news had come out, and no one any longer knew what was going on there. Non-native Iraqis made brief and risky visits, like dives into shark-infested waters. For war correspondents, however, living on adrenaline and scoops, Fallujah was the last frontier.

Why was I so eager to go? The fact is, Fallujah with all its dangers represented precisely why I was covering the war, and why — to the distress of my partner — I kept coming back to Iraq. In Fallujah, I knew I would be the first reporter to meet the very man who embodied evil in the eyes of Americans, the devil's spawn.

So far I had managed to cover and understand both sides of the war. I had been lucky and had often enjoyed rare access to the insurgents, trying always to process and sort out the information I received in the opposing camps. But from the moment the insurgents started using the barbaric tactic of decapitation, my journalistic objectivity faded, leaving me with complete horror and disgust at their archaic fanaticism. What had at first been perceived as resistance had evolved into all-out terrorism. True, barbarism had a way of shifting from one side to another in Iraq.

What was unacceptable for one was quickly explained away by the other. But this time, I had come face to face with absolute otherness. These acts could never be justified. Furthermore, how was it possible that Arab intellectuals, no doubt equally disturbed by these acts that risked tainting the entire Muslim world, had not yet come together to speak out against barbarism? The future of the insurgency was now at stake in Fallujah. The town had become a jumping-off point for the restoration of pride among Islamists. My job was to try and understand the gap between two civilizations.

Which of my convictions, prejudices, elements of my identity as a Western woman, I wondered, would I have to surrender in order to understand them?

I must confess that one of the reasons I wanted to go to Fallujah was a perverted kind of laziness. If this interview was successful, I would no longer have to write the banal political analysis of the transfer of power I had tediously been researching in Baghdad for weeks. This on-the-spot report would preempt it.

But now I was also afraid. Very afraid. What had I got myself into! In my Baghdad hotel, the Korean photographer for *Time*, Cho, pleaded with me every day: Whatever you do, don't go to Fallujah! He had tried using his contacts in the Iraqi resistance to intercede with the kidnappers of Kim Sun Il for the release of his compatriot, but he had failed and Kim had had his throat slit. Cho was still traumatized.

Sitting around the hotel pool, none of the reporters would utter the name of "the F town," even though we all knew it was on everyone's mind. This was especially true after some extremists in Fallujah issued a fatwa authorizing the killing of all foreign reporters. "You're not going *there* today? Don't do anything stupid," my friends would say. Journalism in Iraq is a merciless business, and although a good reporter is a live reporter, none of them wants to lose out on a scoop.

Like my colleagues, I had originally given up on the idea of going to Fallujah. For ten days Yan and I had danced attendance on sheikhs from Fallujah who had taken refuge in Baghdad, drunk tea with them in the hope of getting a safe-conduct, a password, an invitation. In London a Salafist (reactionary militant) doctor I had met and befriended during the siege of Fallujah in April 2004 had given me letters of recommendation in case I was arrested by jihadis, and cryptic passwords. With tears in his eyes, he too had pleaded with me to abandon my expedition. I'd had no better luck in Baghdad. Since spending a few days earlier on with the insurgents who had carried out the first attack on a civilian aircraft in Iraq, the one belonging to DHL, I had established many contacts with anti-American guerrillas, which made me assume that entering Fallujah would be relatively easy. But no one wanted to help me now. Kidnappings had grown far more frequent; I was politely warned that even my "contact" could not guarantee my safety. Much tougher mujahideen had just taken control of the war against American occupiers. I was on my own.

With the decapitation of Nick Berg, the nature of the war had radically changed. In Fallujah's total war against the infidel West, there was no time to make distinctions of nationality or sex. And a detailed account of the death of six Shiite drivers cut into pieces called for a political analysis of the new Iraqi government. Not to mention the fact that, one after the other, all the translators I approached, on the chance I might find a way to be invited into the accursed town, categorically refused, despite their need for money. Was I crazy to pursue going to Fallujah?

Only Muhammad, my driver and guide in Iraq throughout the time I had been covering the war, now accompanied me in Baghdad as I made my rounds to find ways to get to Fallujah. He seemed to be even more frustrated than I by our failure. At night, after dropping me off at my hotel, he went on his own trying to stir up his contacts in Fallujah. I pleaded with him to be careful, knowing how dangerous it was for an Iraqi to act as a go-between. His life was in greater danger than mine, and that responsibility frightened me each day a little more.

On July 23, Muhammad and I finally had a lead. Through a complex set of messengers, I sent my Arabic business card to

someone identified to me as an associate of the leader of the mujahideen in Fallujah. He carried out the customary checks, and
Muhammad told me I had passed the test. This man had vouched
for me. As a guarantee, however, Muhammad had to surrender
his address and the names of all his brothers and cousins, an act
that placed him further on the firing line. We were both on pins
and needles. One false move and his entire family, wife and children, would pay the price.

A few hours later Muhammad's cell phone rang, and I gathered from his respectful tone and his apparent disappointment
that this was the call we had been waiting for. It was bad news,
however. "Do not come under any circumstances. You are not
welcome. We will not guarantee your safety."

My face betrayed my feelings — I wanted to howl in disappointment. All this wait for nothing! Muhammad, deeply distressed, suggested we disregard the warning and visit one of his
friends in Fallujah to get a feeling of the town's atmosphere.

The image, back in April 2004, of the charred leg hanging
from a wire over my head that day in Fallujah flashed back into
my mind, as did the memory of my journalist colleagues who, a
few days later, were forced at gunpoint to lie in the dust. I also remembered my first visit to Fallujah, when a Salafist sheikh had
stepped between me and a gang pointing weapons in my direction. Not to mention Kim, and Nick Berg. No, I would definitely
not go, and I was fully reconciled: it was just too dangerous.

Next morning, however, Muhammad rushed into the hotel
out of breath, in a state of panic. The "people" in Fallujah suddenly requested that we come very early the next day. He didn't
understand, for the rejection had been so categorical the day before. What had made them change their minds? Was this a trap?
We spun out the most complicated theories. Had they seen on
the Internet one of my pieces that displeased them and were
ready to finish me off? Was it my name, my CV? Had Muhammad's insistence made them suspicious? What would happen to
us? Would we ever return?

No, we had to give up the whole idea once and for all. No

article was worth having our throats slit. But we no longer had any choice, Muhammad told me. We simply had to accept the "invitation" and go. If we didn't, the insurgents would take exception. And they not only knew where he lived, they even knew the number of my hotel room.

Muhammad rang my doorbell at six in the morning. His face was drawn; it was clear he had not slept. He inspected me, making sure I was properly dressed — nothing could be left to chance. Muhammad's poise and volubility had been responsible for securing this "invitation." He had spent long hours at the Iraqi game of name-dropping, listing all his religious acquaintances in the region in the hope the mujahideen were related to some of them. Trying to impress them, he had also talked about all the reporting I had done since I had begun covering Iraq, and praised my impartiality. This must have been a good part of the reason the insurgents finally said yes. Being interviewed by a member of the French press made it possible for the insurgents to convey their message to the world. My only safeguard: I was serving their purpose.

Still, we knew there were no guarantees, and as we set off we were deathly afraid. The hard part would be to make it to the house of the people who had agreed to see us. We had at all costs to avoid being intercepted by one of the several roving groups of mujahideen, who might simply shoot at us for the hell of it before taking the trouble to find out whether we had permission to go where we claimed. What's more, how could we be sure the fighters along the way would recognize the authority of the man who had agreed to let us enter the capital of the jihad? The fatwa authorizing the killing of reporters didn't help. American bombing of Fallujah had resumed a few days earlier, and the inhabitants were understandably nervous. Anyone could be considered a spy. Not to mention the patrolling coalition forces, also trigger-happy on this road, the most dangerous road in Iraq.

I put on a headband that completely covered and flattened my hair and a *hijab* that came down to my shoulders. I was wearing a full-length black tunic and, over everything, a long Iraqi *abaya* like the ones worn by Shiite women. I put the recommendations Dr. Salam had given me for the sheikhs of the town into my pants pockets — lists of names and enigmatic code phrases, one of which mentioned "the last bullet of the last battle."

In Muhammad's yellow Chevrolet Caprice, originally a New York taxi, I had always had the impression that everyone was looking at us. But yellow happens to be the color of Baghdad taxis as well, and we were in fact relatively inconspicuous, especially with my Iraqi costume. Sitting next to Muhammad, I could have passed for one of the women in his family. When reporters had begun to be singled out and it had become extremely dangerous to travel in Iraq, being a woman was an advantage.

We were not allowed to bring anyone with us. Yan was very disappointed, but he understood and didn't insist. He knew his presence would put us in even greater danger. Terrified at letting me go alone, he hugged me and stoically said nothing. I was frankly relieved that he couldn't come. It would have been sheer madness for both of us to risk our lives and, literally, abandon our daughter.

I really would have liked at least to take a photographer along. But the insurgents trusted only Muhammad and me, the reporter he had vouched for. I would have to deal with his English, which was not great, though getting better every month. We had no camera, the sign of a spy to the mujahideen, and no satellite phone. Muhammad took along his mobile phone, with the batteries carefully removed so that his car could not be tracked by satellite. Since the "DHL affair," we knew it was impossible to move around Iraq without being noticed.

In the pale light of dawn, we took the road I had already traveled dozens of times, the desert road to Jordan. There were tanks scattered on the roadside and a single Iraqi police checkpoint on the outskirts of the town. I couldn't figure out why Americans didn't have a roadblock on the "hottest" road in Iraq. No one stopped us, and the trip took less than an hour. At that time of day, the streets in the outskirts were deserted. We turned right after the mosque, near the very spot where I had seen the charred leg.

In this particular spot, we knew that we risked being stopped, shot, and decapitated at any moment, and I felt my heart pounding. Nicholas Berg's pleas echoed in my head. But as we moved through town, my fear dissipated. My *abaya* made me invisible and, absurdly, made me feel safe and invulnerable. Outsiders, even Iraqis from the immediate area, were automatically suspect in Fallujah and in danger of death unless they produced a good reason for being there and a proper invitation. The entire town was controlled by totalitarian fanatics who executed people without trial as they saw fit. The mujahideen had become killing machines, impervious to compassion.

We woke up Ahmed, the man who had agreed to let us wait in his house until our point man came to fetch us. His dilapidated house had the advantage of being on the outskirts of town, which made it relatively safe. In the car, Muhammad had outlined the "career" of this man, whom he had met the preceding April while taking photographs of the fighting during the siege of the town.

Strictly speaking, Ahmed did not belong to al-Zarqawi's group, Unification and Jihad, but he sometimes helped out with logistics. For example, one day in January 2004 he went to collect the body of one of the Saudi "martyrs" who had just blown himself up near the Khaldiya Bridge. He told me that he had great admiration for the men who had the courage to become "martyrs," and added, "I, too, when I have run out of weapons, will have no choice but to blow myself up."

Ahmed was extremely thin, with a face swallowed up by a long black beard. He seemed to be suffering from the fierce July heat. Already at this early hour the temperature was above 100°, with no fans, no cold water. In the three months since the April siege, Fallujah had had only two or three hours of electricity a day. Ahmed told us about his skirmishes with the "American devils," and about the hunt for spies, of whom he said there were many in the town. He mentioned a fake beggar woman who went from door to door, whose task was to point out fighters' houses to the coalition forces. "To set an example," he said matter-of-factly, "we had to decapitate and dismember her." Hearing something like that shakes even a seasoned reporter to the core. I had trouble concentrating. The time Muhammad took to translate enabled me to conceal my feelings. I thought about how Yan, back in Baghdad, must be worrying.

At the foot of the couch I was ushered to, I stepped on old Russian Kalashnikovs. With a patronizing smile, Ahmed said, "Those are the children's toys." The only assets of these poor people consisted of weapons, and they learned to shoot as children. "This was a gift from Saddam, although he didn't know it, when he enrolled us all in training camps when we were very young." As though to illustrate his father's words, Ahmed's seven-year-old son skillfully loaded the submachine gun. During the fighting in April, the little boy had helped by keeping a lookout and carrying messages. His mother, her face covered by a long white veil, looked at him with pride. Since the revelations about torture in the American prison of Abu Ghraib, she too had come to think of the decapitation of hostages as rightful vengeance. Looking fondly at her son, she said, "One of my uncles spent more than a year in Abu Ghraib. We will never know if he was tortured or raped. He would rather die than tell us." Then she handed me a piece of paper, a rudimentary CV, asking me to bring it to the government office where she had worked before the war. It may appear paradoxical, but, when they were not fighting Americans or executing spies, insurgents and their wives longed for the orderly life of government employees.

After many phone calls and a few hours spent discussing the jihad and sipping warm, flat soda, we were told that the right-hand man of the head of the Fallujah council of resistance, the dreaded Omar Hadid, had arrived.

The man who entered was in his mid-thirties with a round baby face. His closed and hard look belied the softness of his features.

Muhammad, Ahmed, and I all piled into the car driven by Mazen, Omar Hadid's lieutenant. The radio was playing chanted prayers, the only music now allowed in Fallujah. Proudly Mazen ushered us through his town, controlled by his group. At first frowning, faces brightened as soon as they recognized him. "Who is she?" "She's with me." I felt like a Jew being escorted into Gestapo headquarters by Himmler himself. Reverence was apparent on the faces we saw. Iraqi soldiers were quick to answer his questions. I was being driven by the prince of the town.

Driving through the streets of Fallujah, a "Wahhabi emirate," I saw that the Islamist republic the fundamentalists were calling for in Iraq and elsewhere was beginning to take shape. Between American bombing raids, the town was living under the most rigorous form of Islam. This Islamic showcase was a terrifying Orwellian world. Was it to attain this "paradise," which resembled Saddam's regime with a religious tinge, that the insurgents were fighting here? On the dusty walls, the "decrees of Allah" were posted everywhere: no alcohol, no makeup, no Western hairstyles, and a call to denounce foreigners. The few women we encountered in the street had their faces covered with black crepe veils and wore gloves. I saw Iraqis still living in tents in front of their destroyed houses while others, who had received compensation from the coalition, were busy rebuilding their homes. Life was slowly coming back, but under strict surveillance. The omnipresent mujahideen were obeyed for fear of the harshest punishments.

Mujahideen everywhere had replaced the generals of the former Iraqi army through whom the Americans had thought they would be able to control the most dangerous town in Iraq. At every intersection, Iraqi soldiers and policemen were flanked by mujahideen openly in command. Body language was very eloquent. Power gave the mujahideen a martial presence, while Iraqi soldiers flicked their eyes in fear. "They have to ask our permission to arrest anyone at all," Mazen noted, adding that it was a matter of time before they got rid of the soldiers. "But look at how safe the town is since we have been here. Now we can leave our doors unlocked. And if anyone behaves badly, we execute him."

I nodded. The town seemed to exude fear and denunciation.

Sitting in the backseat, I scrutinized his face. He didn't look like my idea of a religious fanatic. His face was chubby, almost soft. When I told him that, it made him smile, revealing a bitter expression on his lips. Before joining the jihad, Mazen had studied painting, but now he had nothing but contempt for his former passion, a weakness he had to suppress to make himself hard and become a killer.

I observed the town through the windows of the small white car of the lieutenant of the mujahideen. It was swarming with armed men, uniforms, and informers from various insurgent groups. Everyone was spying on everyone else. As we approached the little iron bridge, where barely two months earlier the photographer Stanley Greene and I had seen the charred bodies of American security guards kicked and stabbed by the crowd, two Iraqi National Guard soldiers, red berets nearly covering their eyes, were standing, visibly petrified. They cast worried looks at two white pickup trucks armed with machine guns racing by, with mujahideen brandishing their weapons. Tension in this dangerous spot was electric. "American soldiers were not prepared to lose their lives for Fallujah. We love death as much as they love life," said Mazen.

To hear him tell it, the siege of Fallujah in April was for Iraqi Salafists what September 11 had been for Bin Laden — their first great victory over the American enemy. Mazen, who had participated in negotiations with the coalition forces, claimed that the Americans had given in on almost everything, whereas the Fallujah resistance council ceded nothing. "We did not turn over the men responsible for the death of the four American spies, nor did we surrender our weapons. The Americans had to withdraw their troops, compensate two-thirds of the families, and leave their post in the hospital. They asked us for only one thing: to let them win the media battle. So they filmed their entry into the town, but on Humvees, not tanks as they had asked us." In Mazen's version of events, it was evident that American pragmatism, and the strategy of withdrawal to stop the bloodbath that was beginning to dirty the hands of the coalition forces, had been interpreted by the mujahideen as a sign of weakness.

After about an hour, the car stopped outside a mosque known as a meeting place for anti-American guerrillas. Mazen, the lieutenant of Unification and Jihad, had brought me to Imam al-Janabi. It took him only five minutes to get me an interview with the most influential cleric in the town, the coalition forces' most wanted man. I had not asked for the interview — I would have been too fearful to meet the instigator of hostage assassinations. As I replayed in my mind Nick Berg's video, my throat went dry. While I sometimes managed to blur those pictures, I never completely eliminated them from my memory. A word, a sensation would be enough to make the echo of his agonized begging voice burst through to the surface of my consciousness.

Now in Fallujah I had no say in what went on. I met whoever I was introduced to; I was in the hands of my "hosts." A chill ran down my spine when al-Janabi sat down in front of me. I recognized his face. Some months earlier, before the situation in Fallujah had come to a head, he had been interviewed by several television networks, including al-Jazeera. Since then, he said, he had cut off contact with the media, including the Arab media, which he did not trust. For American soldiers, he was the quintessential bad guy. In the new hierarchy of the mujahideen emirate, the cleric whom Mazen introduced as "the Iraqi Sheikh Yassin" was the political and religious leader of the jihad against Americans. I wanted to understand the infernal logic that led him to justify decapitation. The inhabitants of the town identified him as the leader of the *takfiri*, the most extremist fighters, foreigners or Iraqis tied to foreign Arab organizations. Imam al-Janabi was much younger than Sheikh Ahmed Yassin, the late leader of Palestinian Hamas, but he had the same pepper- and-salt beard, the same sharp features, the same disturbing serenity of a mystic. Without blinking, I knew, he could have ordered our execution.

Muhammad had gone off to pray with the "Arabs." I knew he had not wanted to leave me alone face to face with the irritated imam, but when he was asked to pray — a request that could not be refused in the headquarters of the Wahhabi emirate of Iraq — he had no choice. Without a translator, I sat facing the sharp-featured man who looked at me sternly. I constantly scrutinized my host's facial expressions, trying to determine his attitude toward me. Finally Muhammad returned and the imam began to speak.

Our discussion started with his expressing amusement at the fact that the last letter sent by former American administrator Paul Bremer to Prime Minister Iyad Allawi was a demand for his capture "dead or alive."

Was he afraid of the Americans? I asked.

"In this life, we are but mere tenants, and I hope to see my final dwelling place," he answered.

He had been accused of responsibility for the assassination of six Shiite truck drivers from Baghdad whose mutilated bodies had been returned to their families in exchange for a "mujahideen tax." The imam refused to accept responsibility for those murders, which had created serious tensions between the Shiite and Sunni communities. "We are always executing spies. I would tell you if I had killed them, too."

Under Saddam's dictatorship, the nefarious imam had been barred from preaching for seven years. "I said what I thought of him, just as I now say what I think of the Iraqi prime minister: he's not worth the dust under my feet."

According to the paranoid and egocentric Sheikh al-Janabi, the Americans had invaded Iraq solely in order to launch a "crusade" against Fallujah, the most Islamic town in the country. "Right here they destroyed the gate of the mosque with dynamite, left their shoe prints on the Koran, and spied on our women with binoculars, which for us is worse than death." And the sheikh described the long ordeal of the inhabitants of his town up to the "holy battle of Fallujah": " Then angels on horse-back came down from heaven, weapons kept firing for hours without being reloaded, and spiders emitting noxious odors at-tacked American soldiers, especially the ones who had used their accursed binoculars."

I scrutinized his deep-set black eyes, trying to determine whether the imam believed what he was telling me or whether it was an image, a divine parable. Apparently not, for he went on describing with great attention to detail the hairy legs of the spi-ders that had come to help them against the Americans. I lis-tened, thinking, why not? For me, with no religious education, the story was no more or less strange than the multiplication of loaves and fishes, which some Christians believe literally. Could it be that these people had retained the sense of mystery and magic of early Christians? In this war of religion, each side be-lieves that God is guiding its weapons, the grenade launchers of the insurgents or the M-16s of American soldiers.

While the imam, with great mystical flights, was shaping the supernatural epic tale of the jihad in Iraq, real cries coming from outside shook me out of the hypnotic spell cast by the reli-gious leader. I was in Fallujah, I suddenly remembered, in the in-surgents' mosque surrounded by Arab jihadis who had come from around the world with one goal: to fight against the West of which I was a representative. Oddly enough, I wasn't really afraid. I knew that, although they might slit throats, these people had a keen sense of hospitality, and the fact that I was in a way their guest reassured me. But up to what point? Al-Janabi's entire entourage suddenly rushed out of the room into the courtyard of the mosque, where about forty fighters had gathered, shouting. They were carrying four bleeding and horribly mutilated bodies, which they set on white sheets at the imam's door. The sheets were soon soaked in blood. There I was, in the middle of all of these men who were shooting looks of hatred in my direction. The atmosphere had abruptly changed. Had I not been the "guest" of the imam, I would have been dead. Mazen went out to identify the bodies and returned, devastated and trembling with

anger. Muhammad rolled his eyes, and I could see he was afraid
for me. He offered his condolences to Mazen, who did not acknowledge them. As for Imam al-Janabi, he seemed indifferent
to the hazards of war, and had not cast a glance at the courtyard.
Looking me straight in the eye, he complacently recalled his sermon in 1996 preaching that the Iraqi people would awake from
their lethargy when the United States invaded the country. His
tone became just a touch more excited than at the beginning of
our conversation.

"The day has come; it marks the beginning of the decline of
the American empire, which will tear itself apart for much longer
than Iraq's current ordeal. This is the justice of Allah coming to
earth, bringing down dictators, first Saddam, then Bush and the
Americans. In Iraq, in the United States, wherever they are in
the world, they will be hunted down and destroyed," was the
pronouncement of this Iraqi Bin Laden.

Mazen informed me that we were next going to see the military
leader of the Fallujah resistance council, the emir of the town,
Omar Hadid, known to his lieutenants as the man of steel. Seeing the deference expressed by al-Janabi's entire entourage, I realized I was being taken to the top of the jihadi hierarchy, though
I was not yet aware that I was about to meet the right-hand man
of Abu Musab al-Zarqawi in Iraq.

Abu Musab al-Zarqawi is today, with Osama bin Laden, the
most wanted man in the world. The U.S. government is offering
a $25 million reward for information leading to his capture, the
same amount offered for the capture of Bin Laden before March
2004. This Jordanian-born Salafi Islamist militant of forty is
now the head of al-Qaeda in Iraq. His group was the first to sys-
tematize the kidnappings and beheadings. Al-Zarqawi has al-
legedly confessed, on multiple audiotapes, to having committed
numerous acts of violence in Iraq, including killing civilians and
taking hostages. In 2004, his organization, Jama'at al-Tawhid
wal-Jihad (Unification and Holy War Group, or Unification and
Jihad), claimed responsibility for nine beheadings in six months:

Nicholas Berg in May, South Korean Kim Sun Il in June, Bulgarians Georgi Lazov and Ivaylo Kepov in July, Turks Murat Yüce and Durmus Kumdereli in August, Americans Eugene "Jack" Armstrong and Jack Hensley in September, and Briton Kenneth Bigley in October. On October 21, 2004, al-Zarqawi officially announced his allegiance to al-Qaeda and referred to his own Jama'at al-Tawhid wal-Jihad as "al-Qaeda in Iraq." On December 27, 2004, al-Jazeera broadcast an audiotape of Bin Laden calling al-Zarqawi "the prince of al-Qaeda in Iraq" and asked "all our organization brethren to listen to him and obey him." Then al-Zarqawi left the battlefield, becoming the invisible inspiration of the jihad, following in the steps of al-Qaeda's top leaders, Bin Laden and al-Zawahiri.

Al-Zarqawi violently opposes the presence of U.S., Israeli, and Western military forces in the Islamic world. In September 2005 he reportedly declared "all-out war" on Shiite Muslims in Iraq, and he has already sent numerous al-Qaeda suicide bombers to target areas with large concentrations of Shiite civilians, fueling the civil war that is now spreading in Iraq, although he may not be responsible for all the crimes the American forces accuse him of.

It was now five in the afternoon. We entered a little cement house in the al-Jolan neighborhood that had escaped the heavy bombing in the area. Attacks by the American army had resumed a few days earlier, and I tried to forget that the people whom I was spending the day interviewing might also decide to keep me with them. They too risked being hit by a missile at any moment. In a small sitting room, fifteen of the heads of the most extreme tendency of the mujahideen were gathered around their leader. Omar Hadid, seated before me in a white dishdasha, was about thirty, with a short black beard and an impenetrable expression.

As always when meeting Salafists in Iraq, the conversation inevitably seemed to gravitate toward the place of women in Islam, and the contrast with French secularism. "See how that *hijab* suits you," Hadid said appreciatively, pleased to see I was wearing the traditional long Iraqi *abaya*. "They say that woman in Islam is not the equal of man, but that's a lie. In our eyes, woman is a gem we wish to protect and set in a jewel box." This was the fourth time since I had been in Fallujah that I heard this digression on the precious status of women for Muslims. I smiled politely and said nothing. "If your husband were a Muslim, do you think he would let you take all these risks? You could spend your days lying on a couch watching television," said the brain behind the Fallujah jihadis, no doubt thinking I would go pale with envy. How could a woman have my job, far from her family, exposed to danger? For all the Iraqi men and women with whom I spoke, this was an inexhaustible source of bewilderment. My mind drifted to Yan and his concern, and I thought how lucky I was to have a man like him in my life.

I quickly moved on to the many questions I had about Fallujah. How was the "resistance" to the occupation structured? Who conceived, organized, and coordinated hostage takings as well as attacks? Were some hostages held here?

At that moment, staring at me, he told me he was one of the group of masked assassins I had seen on the video of the murder of Nicholas Berg. I shivered inwardly.

He saw my distress, and it seemed to amuse him. I instinctively touched my neck, no longer feeling much like asking questions. I was afraid of the answers, afraid the killer would regret telling me too much and not let me leave. He urged me on. "Ask whatever you like." Muhammad was very impressed and translated in a loud voice, clearly articulating every word. I asked him to lower his voice.

In the glacial silence following his statement, Omar Hadid asked me what I thought of his combat. How was I supposed to respond to the killer without risking my life? I decided to be as frank as possible.

"Many Westerners understand your desire to free yourself from military occupation. But what we cannot accept, what for us is a symbol of barbarism, is the decapitations," I said, smiling nervously. This provoked general mirth. I think they attributed my disgust to the weakness of my sex. They all assumed a macho pose.

Omar Hadid started to laugh openly. "Watch the video of Berg's decapitation that I gave you twice and, you'll see, you'll get used to it," he advised me. "Why don't you attend the next execution?" he suggested. He was prepared then and there to dispose of one of the prisoners he was holding just to illustrate his point. All around, the mujahideen respectfully listened to their leader justifying to a foreigner the executions that had shocked the entire world. With a weak smile, I declined his invitation.

While Omar Hadid was explaining his "duty to kill," flashes from the video I had watched the night before in the hotel kept coming back to me. The terrible animal cries of Nick Berg echoed in my ears as he lay huddled in agony beneath the relentless attack of his executioners. All the time Omar Hadid was speaking to me, the flood of these inhuman images danced before my eyes. "You know, when we cut off a head, we take pleasure in it," one of the men sitting to the right of the emir explained in English.

A distinct murmur of disapproval greeted the sadistic words of this man. The atmosphere was icy. Omar Hadid put his hand on the man's shoulder and ordered him in Arabic to be quiet. Changing the tone, he chose to talk to us about Safia Bint al-Mutailib, who, during the battle of Mecca against the Jews in 627, had decapitated one of the men attacking her.

"We don't kidnap just to frighten the people we take hostage," Hadid said, in an attempt to be diplomatic, "but to put pressure on countries helping, or about to help, the Americans. What are they thinking, those who are coming into an occupied country? They make deals with the United States to further their commercial interests. But their contracts are stained with the blood of Iraqis. Are we supposed to stand there with our arms folded while we're being assassinated? Cutting someone's head off may not be a good thing. But you have to agree the method works. In battle, Americans tremble in fear. And look at the reaction of the Philippines. Thanks to their withdrawal from Iraq, which enabled us to free our hostage, we were able to show the world that we, too, love peace and mercy. I did try to negotiate an exchange of Nick Berg for Iraqi prisoners. It was the Americans who refused. They're the ones who are really responsible for his death."

Would I be taken hostage? Was I safe here? I asked Omar Hadid.

"Yes," he answered, "as long as your president doesn't send troops to Iraq. If he did, we would have to kill you."

Omar Hadid hated to be reminded that he had been Saddam Hussein's bodyguard. The former dictator had thrown him in prison simply because he belonged to an Islamist party. When he got out, Hadid had tried to go to Afghanistan and join the fight against the Americans. But he missed his rendezvous with the jihad; he arrived too late. The rout of the Taliban caught him on the Iranian border. He had drawn some lessons from the history of Muslim fighters in Afghanistan, he told me. "We understood that division would be our downfall. That's why we set up this council of mujahideen."

Within this council of thirteen military leaders, he had distributed different tasks to each group. Some kept watch on the enemy, others took care of logistical support. Some cut American supply lines and shot at convoys. Still others took charge of kidnapping. As leader, he had one further task: to execute false fighters who used their weapons to terrorize and rob the population of Fallujah. According to Omar Hadid, the end of the siege of Fallujah on April 29, 2004, brought together all the little groups of fighters. "For the Muslim community, the hatred Americans feel for Fallujah has become the symbol of their hatred for Islam," he continued. Since the siege, he said, Fallujah was where negotiations on hostages and decapitations were centralized, Fallujah was where attacks around the country were organized. The next objective was to intensify simultaneous attacks "to show our unity and our strength."

While we were speaking, two leaders of fighting groups,

one from Hoseiba on the Syrian border, and the other from Haditha, 250 kilometers west of Baghdad, had entered the room. After embracing the emir with respect, touching shoulders in the Bedouin manner, they convened a "working" meeting.

Nothing exasperated Iraqi Salafist mujahideen more than asking them if foreign fighters, the ones they called "the Arabs," had taken control of the struggle. "That's an American lie," Hadid answered bitterly. "We Iraqis are in command of our town and are planning resistance in the country. 'Arab' fighters have come to help us. Fallujah has become a symbol for all Muslims, the starting point for the reconquest. So we welcome them, why not? Americans have their allies, don't they?"

I expressed surprise: in the DVD of the operations of Unification and Jihad that the military leader had sent me a few days earlier in Baghdad, most suicide bombings filmed had been carried out by these "foreign fighters."

"Yes," he answered, "because becoming a *shahid* is the supreme act of faith. Iraqis have not yet reached that degree of fervor. But they are slowly beginning to imitate their 'Arab' brothers." The emir was dismayed to acknowledge that Arab support troops still had lessons in faith to offer to his compatriots.

Though I had been asked not to mention the name of the Jordanian jihadi, I nonetheless braved the question: "And Abu Musab al-Zarqawi, Bin Laden's Jordanian lieutenant — is he the one who plans all the attacks, as the Americans believe?"

"There is no Zarqawi in Fallujah. Elsewhere? He is probably somewhere in Iraq. But the most important thing is that in Fallujah today we are all Zarqawis, and Iraqis are all Bin Ladens."

"And when will you stop fighting?"

"When the occupation is over and Islamic law is established in Iraq. Until then, no Muslim country in the world will know peace."

The interview was over. Before showing us out, Omar Hadid insisted on transmitting a solemn message to Jacques Chirac and George Bush: "We will kidnap all citizens of nations allied with the United States and the infidel government of Iraq. We will decapitate citizens of nations who refuse to reconsider their support for our enemies. Whoever helps our enemy becomes our enemy. The Vietnamese also cut off heads during their war with the United States. You can't say that we haven't warned you."

This was war, and he demanded an eye for an eye, no more and no less.

Eager for a final example of the "barbarism" of his enemies, he went on to say that the bloody bodies I had seen in the mosque had not only been filled full of bullets but had had their throats cut by American soldiers. He offered to show them to me. Could American soldiers have decapitated the bodies in order to send a message to the insurgents, and out of a desire to avenge the desecration of their comrades' bodies? Since the video of Nick Berg's decapitation, the affair of the Abu Ghraib tortures, the arrest of Saddam Hussein, and the live broadcast of his medical exam, this war had become a war of symbols. Humiliation had become the number one weapon. We went back to the mosque, but the bodies were gone and we headed for the cemetery.

And then, suddenly, this macabre chase disgusted me. What had I learned in the course of this dangerous day? That the throat slitters acted in the name of God, that they justified their barbarity by abuse against them at the hands of the Americans? That Islamism, like Christian fundamentalism, like all religions pushed to the extreme, is a sectarian and sterile form of indoctrination? Suppose everything was nothing but a matter of one's viewpoint. In a way, I envied those convinced they held the truth, decreed good and evil, and could tell the good guys from the bad. It made things so simple. Dangerously simple. I was drained of emotions. Night was falling; it was time to go back to Baghdad.

On the road, Muhammad was as exhilarated by having pulled off our "interview" as I was weary, and he was driving much too fast, which risked making the American soldiers on this heavily monitored road, who were already nervous, even more trigger-happy. I suggested he slow down. Being criticized by a woman was hard for him, and he lost his temper. All at once, we started shouting at each other as we never had before, and he swore it was the last time he would work for me. It was pure tension, and we both knew it. We made up soon after, drinking very sweet lemon tea from Basra in a restaurant where Yan joined us on our return to Baghdad. Ignoring repeated warnings that it was not wise to stop in a public place so late, I sat down, utterly exhausted. I had no desire to go back to the hotel and face my night demons. During the first months, I managed to control my fears somehow during the day, but at night anxiety would inevitably resurface and I would wake up drenched in sweat.

I had to call my magazine. "You want the cover?" said one of my editors, sounding doubtful. The intended cover was to be about the passion for gardening, an issue that would bring in many advertising pages. Wouldn't I settle for a reference on the cover? Since the DHL affair, I had gained some credibility as a war reporter. If I were writing for an American periodical, the question would not even have arisen: my interview with Omar Hadid would have been instant front page. But in France, interest in the Iraq war had already faded. It was not their war, and most French were against it. Still, my editor would have to trust me. I couldn't be more explicit. A few words were all I was able to whisper. My phone and Muhammad's were probably tapped. Jumpy, speaking low, I was looking over my shoulder, trying to make sure no one was watching me. I was afraid of everybody being arrested and questioned by coalition soldiers, of being seized by mujahideen who had had second thoughts about granting me that interview. Paranoia was the name of my new game. And this call had reminded me that I would soon be going home. I would have to face the horrible first days, with jet lag and the inevitable schizophrenia, a feeling that I was returning from a planet no one wanted to hear about. They were right: war is not an easy or attractive subject of conversation. Fortunately, this time there would be two of us to confront the terror of homecoming, of having to recount to friends and colleagues stories no one wanted to hear.

Only on the steps of the hotel did I finally calm down, for it was time to call my daughter, as I did every night. Her sweet, high-pitched voice made everything sound suddenly positive. I told her an animal fable to put her to sleep. The machine guns stuttering in the distance no longer made me jump. She didn't want to hang up. I was happy; I would soon see her again. I also called my parents and my best friend Laurent, to whom I lied as always: "No, I took no risks; in fact, I hardly ever leave the hotel." Only later would they learn the truth, when they read my articles.

It was impossible to sleep. At one in the morning, I went down to swim a few laps in the pool. Two young Americans in civilian clothes, who it turned out were working for the Department of Defense, came up to me and introduced themselves. One of them spoke passable Arabic, unusual for an American. What did the French government have in mind? they asked. Were we finally ready to collaborate with the Americans? Could I informally introduce them to the French ambassador in Iraq? The ambassador had told me he had tried to see Bremer on several occasions without success, I said, and, I was sure, would be happy to talk to them. This said, I explained to them that I was only a reporter and did not represent the French government. Did they think I was part of the French secret service? Were they even aware I had just interviewed al-Zarqawi's lieutenant? Not once did they mention my reporting. What ensued was a completely surrealistic conversation about my degree of patriotism and the chances of bringing our two countries together to collaborate in the war. One of the two had had a few whiskeys. I couldn't tell whether he was flirting or trying to get information from me. What a strange, frightening, surreal day.

Omar Hadid died in the second battle of Fallujah in November 2004. In January 2005 a message attributed to al-Zarqawi paid homage to his "trusted lieutenant." It was only when I read the contents of this message in a Jordanian newspaper that I became fully aware, six months after we met, of the full importance of the man I had interviewed.

2

The War Without a Name
March 2003

THE DAY THE WAR BEGAN, on March 20, 2003, I was in Tehran on my way to Iraqi Kurdistan. The plan for covering the war established months earlier by my magazine, *Le Nouvel Observateur:* one reporter was being sent to Baghdad, one to Kuwait, and I to Kurdistan in northern Iraq.

The Kurdish enclave could be reached only through Iran or Syria, because Turkey had closed its border with Iraq. When the attack began, my friend Jabbar Hussein, the Iraqi writer, called me in a state of both excitement and depression, solemnity and gaiety, optimism and despair. I understood his confused feelings, because I shared them. Ever since the September 11 attacks, Jabbar had been predicting war would come. He was acquainted with the opposition figures living in London and had introduced them all to me, as well as passing along the latest news circulating among the Iraqi diaspora. For him, the invasion meant that he could return to a country and a family he had left more than twenty years before, see again his brothers, his sister, his friends, and the landscapes of his novels. Three years before the American invasion, his beloved mother had died in his absence. A year before the war, I had slipped away from my Baath Party minders in Najaf to photograph her grave for him.

He was afraid for his country about to be invaded, foreseeing the consequences of the war. He was wary of the effects of occupation, even more wary of its critics. His pride as an Iraqi was wounded by the invasion, and he feared that the world he had

built for himself in exile would be shattered. He was like a prisoner who is about to be liberated after a lifetime behind bars but
holds back: he was afraid to measure his dream against reality.

It was Jabbar, his novels, and his passion for the history of his
country from ancient times that had initiated me to Iraq. When
he and I went to see Iraqi exiles in London, I felt as though the effects of the torture he had suffered in Saddam's jails grew deeper.
His contact with fellow Iraqis revived memories buried deep in
his flesh. He had confessed his pessimism about the exile "opposition" to Saddam's regime, fragmented into a plethora of parties,
all vying for a piece of power in the coming Iraq.

From my last visit to Iraq I knew that, like Jabbar, most of
the population was praying for the fall of Saddam's regime. I was
also aware of the Iraqis' fierce nationalism and their distrust of
the Americans. If America's plan was to succeed in Iraq, the United
States could afford to make few if any mistakes.

Seeing pictures of bombs falling on Baghdad that day, I
feared for my friends in Iraq, yet I could not help rejoicing for
them. Perhaps this "unjust" war, undertaken for the wrong reasons, might end up making them free.

The door from Iran to Iraq was just a simple rusted iron gate set
in the rugged snow-covered mountains of Kurdistan. I was surprised, having imagined that the border would be as heavily
guarded as Fort Knox. There was no hint of concrete barriers or
barbed wire. We were five reporters standing before the portal
leading to the Iraq war. The taxi driver who had brought us here
hurried back whence he came, leaving us shivering in front of the
gate, which remained closed. The Iranian bureaucracy had mis-
placed our passes, and the fax machine in the little mountain border post wasn't working, or maybe there was no one at the other
end — no one knew.

I shared a taxi with Stephan, an American freelance reporter
who had worked for *Time* and was now working for *Newsday*.
After several hours of waiting at the gate, we were finally allowed
through. But we still had several hours ahead of us before arriv-

ing at Irbil, one of the "capitals" of Kurdistan. As we drove through the spectacular mountain landscape exchanging ideas, we realized we were complementary rather than competitive. He could help me tone down or keep in perspective the French attitude toward the Americans and this war, and I with my knowledge of the Near East would help him understand the Arabs as we moved toward Baghdad. We decided to team up for the duration of the war. Stephan was competent and courageous, and I have fond memories of our odyssey through Iraq at war. In love with a hot-blooded Italian woman, he was constantly talking to her on our satellite phone. It became our running joke, and I took a picture of Stephan crouched behind a wrecked tank shouting in Italian into his phone. I was madly gesturing to keep him from stepping into minefields in Kurdistan with the phone glued to his ear.

In Irbil we encountered the inevitable media circus that comes with every conflict: swarms of reporters, jammed hotels, inflated prices. After a few nights in the Shirin Palace, a dump unfit for human habitation where reporters slept head to foot, sometimes on the floor, in tiny rooms plunged in darkness, we left and found a room in the Irbil Tower. As in every war, reporters were soon turned into homeless, and the difficulty of washing and bathing, plus our lack of privacy, made us all look disheveled and weird. The only international radio station on at all hours in the Irbil Tower was the audio from Fox TV, because they had set up shop in the hotel. Every night we fell asleep to the sound of Bill O'Reilly's voice or of some peroxide blond anchor introducing experts or presenting complacent reports on a war that we were about to experience in a very different way. The floor occupied by Fox was immediately recognizable. It was a fortified camp with hundreds of sandbags in the hotel corridor. In the middle of the city, when the likelihood of Saddam's army, which had other things on its mind, invading Iraqi Kurdistan was minuscule, and in a place where everyone was in favor of the invasion, Fox was at war. It looked like a movie set. An armed guard kept anyone from getting near, which reinforced the feeling we had throughout the conflict that we were witnessing a spectacle orchestrated to sway public opinion.

The atmosphere prevailing among reporters in Irbil was odd. They had been prepared to cover Pearl Harbor, and were stuck on a front going nowhere. Some of them were prepared for everything and had installed tanks of disinfectant in the trunks of their jeeps to decontaminate their NBC suits in case of a biological or chemical attack.

I received strange looks when I mentioned I hadn't taken my NBC suit out of its blister pack or tried on my gas mask. As for Stephan, he had come without a bulletproof vest. We finally found one for him in the bazaar in Irbil. The plates on his new bulletproof jacket were much lighter than mine, and it was covered in military camouflage cloth. He quickly had it covered in blue cloth, like the vests worn by BBC reporters. Despite all this, he nonetheless managed to look like a hippie who had wandered into the war zone.

We were lucky when it came to our translator, Ferhad. While most reporters struggled with the rudimentary French or English of their guides, we found a doe-eyed Kurd from Kirkuk who had spent almost ten years in Canada and spoke polished English. He had only one minor problem — he hated war. And he warned us that he was not prepared to go just anywhere. With Saddam gone, he had no desire to die just when he was about to see his family and his city again.

A few days after my arrival, the war started here in the north as well. My driver, who rang me on my satellite phone, told me that at the front at Kalak, a Kurdish border post, there had been an exchange of fire. Since Iraqi Kurdistan had won its autonomy in 1991, the dictator's soldiers had surveyed Kalak from the nearby hills, and now their threatening figures were exposing the village to their bullets.

That night, despite American instructions to the contrary, Kurdish fighters took advantage of the retreat to take the offensive. The northern front had moved. We were now in the war. News spread from Kurdish mobiles to our satellite phones.

Arriving at Kalak at around six in the morning, I witnessed an incredible scene. Crouched in the lush grass, the Kurdish fighters, called *peshmerga*, had assembled and were quietly counting their dead under the gaze of American Special Forces. No one was supposed to know that there had been any fighting here. Officially, the northern front had not been opened. Turks assembled their forces on the border, and did not want Kurds to participate in the fighting. *Peshmerga* were whispering that fighting was now going on around the village of Khazar, barely twelve miles from Mosul, less than six miles from where we were standing. Everyone was ecstatic; *peshmerga* and journalists fed up with waiting were rejoicing.

We set out on foot, vehicles being forbidden on the front lines. I had not brought my bulletproof vest — which weighed more than thirty pounds and was too big for me, since it was made for a man — and was pleased not to have to carry that weight. About fifteen photographers, a handful of reporters, thirty *peshmerga*, and a few American Special Forces constituted our group as it set out toward the fighting. Everyone was happily chatting, walking on the country road. The weather was fine, and the deep green grass covered with poppies was an invitation to lie down. We looked as though we were on our way to a picnic.

A Kurdish general with an imposing mustache led the *peshmerga* toward the new front line. Like his men, he too looked delighted. "We're finally going to win back our land." Glancing at the dozen American soldiers with them, he hastened to add: "But we'll wait for American orders."

Special Forces halfheartedly tried to rein in their allies' enthusiasm. "Why are you in such a hurry?" sighed an American officer.

"OK, go ahead, and if you're shot at we'll cover you."

"What about you? Are you in such a hurry to die?" Sergeant John asked me. In this friendly atmosphere, I paid no attention

to his warning, taking it as a joke. There is nothing like the euphoria of a front line moving forward. It reminded me of the
festive atmosphere in Afghanistan, when my fellow reporters
were killed. We had been laughing uproariously, convinced that
bombs were meant only for the others, just like in the movies,
when the unreal vision of Pierre's body was hurled against a
tank . . .

A veteran of the Gulf War, Sergeant John was glad to be
here. He understood the enthusiasm of his Kurdish allies and
pardoned their disorganization. "The *peshmerga* are good fighters: they know both infantry and guerrilla tactics."

Suddenly, amid all this forced gaiety, shots rang out on the
road just in front of us. Iraqi soldiers had opened fire, and I immediately lost sight of the American officer who had warned us
earlier. His arms loaded with the long tubes of two portable
grenade launchers, he had vanished into the ditch on the front
line. Everyone had scattered, and I found myself alone, terribly
alone. Bent over, I raced along the embankment, seeking shelter
next to a Kurdish fighter.

"Those bastards are resisting. We're holding one end of the
bridge, and they're holding the other," explained the *peshmerga*,
who had been fighting on the outskirts of Khazar and had just
withdrawn for a brief respite. Out to capture the village located
on the other side of the bridge, Iraqi soldiers had been ordered
to hold this road between Kirkuk and Mosul, the two cities
which it was said held half the Iraqi army.

Just then, reinforcements from Saddam's army arrived from
Mosul. I could see them clearly with the naked eye, in pickup
trucks heading for the Kurdish lines. With their GPS receivers,
Americans guided the F-18 fighter-bombers, and in the course of
fifteen minutes I saw ten clouds rise over the plain. I found myself smack in a front-row seat for the war. In fact, the front lines
were so close that a trifling error in direction would be enough
for Americans to slaughter their own ranks.

From the radio of one of the *peshmerga* commanders could

be heard the voice of a Kurdish leader who, two days later, was seriously wounded by an American firing error. "Don't shoot first."

Under shelling, the commander's order seemed to me totally incongruous. They were letting themselves be shot at without doing anything? But orders were strict: Kurds must not attack.

"The resistance is fierce. We have to defend ourselves," retorted one of the fighters to his commander over the radio.

Stephan chose to remain in the ditch, while I decided to withdraw a few yards back and continue questioning Kurdish fighters with Ferhad. Just then, a flare landed next to me on the road. I stopped short at the lower end of a little bridge set over a large sewer pipe. Shells kept landing nearer and nearer, and my backpack was covered with rubble thrown up by their impact. Where should we take shelter? three or four of us reporters asked a Kurdish fighter, who looked just as much at a loss as we did. "Why did she come so far to die here?" he asked Ferhad, pointing at me, genuinely puzzled. We finally crouched down and crawled inside a pipe. Inside, huddled together, we listened to the terrible sound of bombs, whose roar was so loud that it felt as though some had penetrated the cylinder encompassing us. All of a sudden, I bitterly regretted getting myself into this mess. The notion of dying on a very secondary front, in a town with an unpronounceable name, in a war that didn't even have the right to call itself one, hit me as being an utter waste and unpardonably stupid. My mouth was dry with fear, my throat so parched it hurt. I wasn't thinking about the bombs or about my family that I would never see again: all I could think of was two sips of water.

Inside the pipe, an American photographer collapsing under her equipment suffered an attack of claustrophobia. It wasn't safe there anyway, we decided, and we started running with our heads down. From his ditch, Stephan had joined us. My legs felt like lead. Taking my backpack, Ferhad dragged me by the arm. Some English reporters who had arrived by car a few hours after us were now leaving in a big hurry to get away from the shelling. Hopping on board, we clung to their doors, our feet on the running boards. Ferhad was on the rear bumper. A few dozen yards down the road, the driver stopped and we all piled into a jeep. Less than a week in Kurdistan, and I had already risked my life in a war without a name.

In the ensuing days, we returned to "make the rounds" of the front lines in the region, hoping to capture again a little of the earlier euphoria when Iraqi soldiers had retreated for the first time. But Saddam's soldiers resisted for several days at the bridge in Khazar. So, to overcome the frustration of being stuck and immobilized while Baghdad was on the verge of being liberated, some reporters took more and more risks to provide colorful dispatches about the war for their impatient editors. Bit by bit, reporters lost all sense of proportion, taking risks completely out of line with any tales brought back from the battlefront. Unknown Iraqi locales became more familiar to war correspondents than the battles of Jena and Austerlitz; they were fortresses to be captured, which we approached as though to measure each other's audacity.

The most foolish reporters I encountered in the north were the French. At night they would relate with excitement the impact of mortar shells that had driven them back. Every day they got a little closer, driven by the adrenaline of war, making fun of deskbound reporters who covered the war from a distance. For them, it seemed all about confronting the winds of war, intoxicated with recklessness. As for me, I was haunted by the memory of my reporter friends who had died in Afghanistan. I remembered the little room we shared when I returned from Fayazabad in northern Afghanistan. We had had nothing to eat except the nauseating rice the Northern Alliance sparingly distributed in buckets. Pierre was fed up with waiting, frustrated at recording for his radio station the muffled and distant rumble of the B-52 bombs over and over again. The euphoric day when the Taliban retreated, he had climbed onto a tank with his colleagues, sharing the exultation of the Northern Alliance's impending victory. At that very moment, the Taliban counterattacked. Bodies were brought back on a tank, without even a sheet to cover them. Pierre was gone.

Reporters on the northern front in Iraq took even more risks, especially women, including Catherine Monnet of Radio France International and Deborah Pasmantier of the Agence France-Presse, the first reporters to venture into Tikrit, Saddam's family seat. I remember their triumphant air as they sat smugly in the café next to the equestrian statue of Saddam. After spending the night in the home of local citizens, they had arrived almost simultaneously with the marines. No one knew who they were. They made fun of tellers of tales, machos who bragged about the war that they were simply experiencing.

I had wanted to go back to this little Kurdish town deserted by the Baathists, which harbored a large community of Yazidis, to interview their leader. These Zoroastrians, whose steepled temples seemed out of a *Star Trek* episode, had had to compromise with a regime that had long oppressed them. But I was forced to change plans. Stephan called, telling me Kirkuk was about to fall. The distance was great, and we had to travel in the opposite direction. Ferhad, our sophisticated translator, hesitated. He was eager to see his family again, especially his father, whom he had not seen for twelve years. But he was afraid, afraid of the Arabs in the city, afraid of snipers. His wife, a beautiful brunette with long hair, pleaded with him not to go. These scenes depressed and weakened him. Ignoring his wife's sobs, Ferhad decided finally to go with us.

When we approached Kirkuk, the city everyone in Iraq coveted, Ferhad exclaimed in delight, "The aroma of Kirkuk," breathing in with pleasure the air filled with nauseating gasoline odors. His happiness made me smile, momentarily distracting me from the chaotic spectacle of war. Through him, I felt what all Kurds were feeling. According to Ferhad, this bitter, suffocating odor came not only from the ditches, where heavy oil had been set alight by the Iraqi army to prevent American planes from seeing their targets, or from the two oil wells in flames giving off thick clouds of purple smoke. He described this odor as the soul of his city, a city he had not seen for a dozen years.

As we continued on the road to Kirkuk, I increasingly had the impression I was watching a war movie in slow motion. In the magnificent meadows of Kurdistan strewn with poppies, the scene I was witnessing — surrealistic — was of inhabitants taking apart bomb-shattered taxis still burning, inside which lay the corpses of Iraqi soldiers who had tried to flee.

At the last checkpoint before the city, we passed pickup trucks already coming back from Kirkuk loaded with booty, while going in our direction were trucks filled with armed *peshmerga* shooting in the air. Hundreds of immobilized cars were honking their horns. Traffic was regulated by Kalashnikov. The noise was terrifying. A scene of hell. No one was taking care of the wounded. A man approached our car. A sniper's bullet had shot off a piece of his cheek. His shirt was drenched with blood dripping onto the ground. "One of Saddam's fedayeen did this to me because I'm a Kurd," he told me, showing his gaping wound. As I was wondering how to give him first aid, he was swallowed up in the crowd. Ferhad, oblivious, was not listening to me. "See how beautiful it is," he whispered, taking me by the arm, looking off in the distance at the approaching city. "The refineries . . . There's my school, Abul Malik. And look, behind the burning tank, that's the house where I was born." Out of chaos, Ferhad was finding his own internal order.

At the entrance to the city, the confusion was total. Girls were offering pastry to the *peshmerga*, chanting: "Long live George Bush." One thing was certain: Americans were heroes here as nowhere else in Iraq. Several buildings were on fire. I didn't know which way to turn, and heard gunshots from every direction. Was it celebration or revenge? One was almost as lethal as the other, and as terrifying. In the governor's palace, five American soldiers were searching men with their backs to the wall, their hands on their heads. There were about fifteen of them, looking at us with a stunned air; they had come from Sudan, Yemen, or Palestine to help Saddam's army. I remember the intensity of their fiery gaze, their air of defiance, which contrasted so deeply with my memory of the beaten air of the Taliban when they were taken prisoner.

As Ferhad got closer to the Kurdish quarter where his parents' house was located, his anxiety increased. We drove around and around the streets of his neighborhood, unable to find the house. About to give up, all of a sudden he saw his father at the doorway of a little house. He had aged, Ferhad said, but there he stood, ramrod straight, despite the years, the exiles, and the separations. I watched father and son standing awkwardly face to face, their eyes full of tears, embarrassed by the deep emotion overwhelming them both. Very soon, fortunately, neighbors swarmed into the house to welcome the exile. An old woman from Halabja, who had been subjected to the gas attack by the Iraqi army in 1988, raised her arms to heaven, thanking God and George Bush. Still, she was afraid that Saddam would come back, as he had in 1991.

The neighbors brought Ferhad up to date about the "devil" of the neighborhood, a man he had constantly talked to me about, the head of the local Baath Party, the terrible Abu Khaldun. This apparatchik had forced young men to join the army and obliged women to clean party headquarters without pay. He had also been the one in charge of the Arabization of Kirkuk, driving out any Kurds who had not been there for many generations. "Our sons took care of him," one neighbor rejoiced. "Our oldest son was the lucky one to kill him," said another quietly.

At every intersection of the city, people begged me to lend them my satellite telephone, and I was delighted to help them out in my small way. They called family members to whom they had in some cases not spoken for years. They cried in relief, reassured their families, rejoiced in the fall of the despot. It was marvelous to witness these people weeping for once with happiness. This was the enthusiasm, and welcome, American soldiers must have expected everywhere in the country. And I have to say that after what I saw during my last visit to Iraq, when Saddam was still ruling the country, I was expecting a greater display of relief, even in the south. But after this succession of tragedies, wars, and oppression, people knew better than to rejoice too soon.

3

Tikrit, Mosul, and the Border
May 2003

S TILL IN THE THICK OF THE WAR, I was dispatched to Tikrit to report on Saddam Hussein's stronghold. Tikrit was the only town in Iraq that had not fallen to the coalition forces. Following rumors that marines were nearby, our small group of journalists had organized a convoy to get us closer to the town. Worried, our three vehicles stopped every five hundred yards to question drivers coming from the opposite direction about the state of security on the road. Not only were there looters all over the roads, but peasants in villages often shot at cars as they drove through. We had made sure to remove our Kurdish license plates that morning, along with the flag stickers and Kurdish banners that our patriotic driver had unthinkingly plastered all over our jeep. The idea of journalistic neutrality was foreign to him. All our drivers and translators were terrified. Ferhad, whose English was excellent but who was not exactly a shining example of bravery, undermined everyone's courage by describing in detail the certain death awaiting us. Every time we stopped, he pleaded with us to turn back. At one stop, discussion among the drivers became heated — it appeared that the marines had not yet entered the town and we were now very close to it. An American photographer started to yell: "This is crazy. Do you know how many friends I've lost pulling stupid stunts like this?" I agreed with him. But I have to confess that the idea of witnessing the historic moment when Saddam's town changed hands, and capturing the atmosphere in the dictator's fortress that had haunted

Iraqis for so long, was sorely tempting. What a scoop it would be
to get to Tikrit before crowds of reporters and soldiers transformed the town by their very presence. Still, our job is not to
place ourselves between two belligerent forces; that would be irresponsible. In any event, Ferhad decided for me: he declared
that we would not go a step farther. Besides, that night I had to
write my account of the fall of Kirkuk, and I wasn't going to take
reckless chances and risk missing my deadline. Since the recent
loss of two of my friends in Afghanistan, I knew better. The excitement of being in the heart of danger was ephemeral. Then
there was the absurdity of dying for a war that, despite my many
years' involvement, was after all not my war. Stephan found a
spot in the car ahead of us that was going a few miles farther, to
the outskirts of the town. I gave him my bulletproof vest and
wished him luck.

When I got back to the jeep, Ferhad had put on the last bulletproof vest and taken a seat in the back, "because snipers shoot
the front passenger first," he said. Nice thought. His attitude was
not attractive, but understandable: why should he die for a bunch
of reporters? He looked pale sitting in the back; usually so talka-
tive, he didn't say a word on the way back to Kirkuk. The atmosphere in the jeep became miserable. Our driver began berating
Ferhad because of his attitude; Ferhad kept stubbornly silent;
and I was worried sick about Stephan. I also knew that Ferhad
felt guilty for exposing me on the front seat; slightly miffed, I
couldn't help making him feel cowardly during those three hours
on the road back to Kirkuk, and that didn't please him. I sensed
that that night he was going to quit, which he did. When we arrived in Tikrit two days later, after finally unearthing the last
"Arab" translator in Kirkuk, the town had already been occupied
by marines for many hours. On the way into town, marines had
us surrender our weapons in exchange for a ticket, like checking
coats in a theater. On the way out of town, everyone could re-
trieve his arsenal. They must have regretted being so permissive.
That was when I discovered that our driver was carrying in his
trunk a revolver, a Kalashnikov, and dozens of boxes of bullets. I

was furious: I had explained to him endlessly that reporters were not supposed to carry weapons. Doing so would put us in grave danger. He nodded, but I knew he really had said yes simply to pacify me. Besides, as the fighting went on, more and more reporters, particularly English and American, did hire armed escorts, some of whom went so far as to carry concealed weapons.

The center of town was practically deserted and eerily quiet, as though everyone was holding his breath waiting for something to happen. The inhabitants, terrified of talking to strangers in Saddam's fortress, skulked along the walls. A small group of people approached us. "Could you ask the American soldiers to destroy the statue of Saddam on horseback?" they asked us. They didn't dare do it by themselves. Suddenly a white car came screeching up, and mustachioed men inside abused and threatened them: "We heard you and we'll find you when all this is over." These men gave me a chill, bringing back the terror that had reigned in Iraq under Baath Party minders in Saddam's time.

Without warning, there was a gigantic roar, and we hit the dirt. Was the war starting up again? American helicopters were blowing up ammunition dumps, and the explosions were intense. At a street corner a little farther along, a kid from Texas who couldn't be more than eighteen asked me in a shaky voice: "Is it really true, miss, that the war is over?" He looked so young, so frail and innocent, despite all his cumbersome equipment. No one had told him anything; in fact, the rank and file often know least about troop movements. I reassured him, handing him my satellite phone so he could call his mother. The phone distorted his voice, and she didn't recognize it at first. "I'm fine, Mom," the young soldier said through his tears in the streets of Tikrit.

We took a tour of Saddam's palaces — or what was left of them — follies in concrete that, it was immediately apparent, were designed to impress the population and affirm the terror inspired by the Iraqi president. Saddam's palaces called up thoughts of Bluebeard's castle, and if you tried to imagine all the tortures inflicted in them, you would still fall short of reality. The most surprising aspect, when you got inside one of these palaces, was the extraordinary ugliness of the construction and furnishings. Bombs had just demolished a good part of the palaces, and we made our way carefully through the rubble. There were gaping holes everywhere in the floors, and flights of stairs leading nowhere. We often had to backtrack in order to find a passable corridor. We moved about like kids exploring an abandoned building in the woods, and tiptoed down to the basement, where we had to use flashlights. In front of a huge empty swimming pool, I encountered a soldier trussed up like a ninja turtle contemplating the blue-painted hole. "My whole apartment would fit in half that pool," he sighed. Like the Iraqi population, he was struck by the flashy luxuriousness of the palace in contrast to the inhabitants' abysmal poverty.

As for me, I was disappointed, having imagined that palaces like this one contained more luxurious megalomania. The furniture, plywood spray-painted gold, looked like it had been bought at Wal-Mart. The only luxurious element of this concrete and gold building was its size. It was an empty shell merely designed to flaunt the dictator's dominance. Some reporters couldn't resist spending the night in beds in which the despot, perhaps, they imagined, had slept. Camping there had no attraction for me. It was clear that Saddam had not worked in these offices, nor had he washed in these bathrooms. These palaces were empty façades.

For the population, however, they represented the formidable setting of the dictatorship that had haunted their nightmares for decades. Some Iraqis, overcoming their initial inhibition, were entering tentatively, in small groups, the forbidden sanctum. Everyone took a souvenir: a doorknob, an Arabic translation of Mao's little red book, sheets, or towels. Our Kurdish driver had disappeared in the palace wearing my bulletproof vest, exploring every corner, examining every shard of glass fallen from the chandeliers, as though he were examining Bluebeard's secret chamber. His amazement, still tinged with fear, was touching.

Stephan and I decided to head back to Mosul, where we heard unrest was brewing. We couldn't travel at night, and had to factor into our journey extra time for detours on blocked or reputedly dangerous roads. Before starting off, Stephan called his Italian girlfriend on his satellite phone for the fifth time that day. She was clearly making a scene, and in this landscape of war, most incongruously, he was shouting for all to hear in Italian and waving his arms like windmills. I wanted to grab the phone and ask her if she couldn't give my colleague a little break, just this once until the war was over. But I didn't. I, who sang lullabies to my daughter while standing on all the roadsides in Iraq, was in no position to give lessons to anyone. In the street, a child offered me a rose. Tikrit continued to be stunned and eerily calm. No one at the time could have predicted the conflagration of the Sunni Triangle and the attacks that would spread throughout Iraq a few months later.

When we reached Mosul, insurrection was in full swing. Frightened colleagues we met on the way out had just been assaulted by inhabitants who greeted them with iron bars and grenades. Riots are often more dangerous than actual wars; attacks can pop from any direction. In the city, faces filled with hatred confronted us with each step we took. I managed to duck into a small café. The crowd was swelling, tension was rising; it didn't look good. I laboriously explained in my poor Arabic who I was and why I was there, drawing on all the vocabulary I had learned the year before in my Arabic course at the Sorbonne. It had the effect I hoped. Tension immediately relaxed, I was lucky — French were looked on favorably here. A man named Ahmed al-Khayat introduced himself as a "businessman" and offered to escort me around Mosul to spare me from getting a bad impression of his city. We zigzagged between overturned burning cars and looted merchandise spread out on sidewalks. In the Datsun pickup in front of us, a little coffin made of rough wood was bouncing up and down. It was a child's coffin with the parents holding on to it, their faces contorted in sorrow. Sadly, not an unusual sight in Iraq. Men in the procession driving at top speed toward the Mosul cemetery raised their fists, yelling: "Is this American democracy? The war of liberation?" I understood, and felt uncomfortable at being associated with one of the most embarrassing foul-ups in Operation Iraqi Freedom: for two days running, American soldiers in Mosul had shot into the crowd, at passersby, at children, why, I didn't know. There had been fifteen killed and several dozen wounded: the most unfortunate outcome of the marines' reaction to riots shaking the city.

Ahmed brought us to Saddam Hospital in Mosul, where his brother was head surgeon. Dr. Muzahim al-Khayat, overwhelmed, could only deal with the most urgent cases. Operations were crude, and there was no longer any anesthetic, nor any kind of medications. "Yesterday the marines shot to kill, today they aimed at the legs," said the surgeon in a professional manner. I passed by the bed of a twenty-year-old man: Othman had been carrying an Iraqi flag in his hands when the Americans opened fire. His leg had just been amputated — too late, according to one of the nurses. The young man was dying. In the next bed was Jabbar Ahmed Ibrahim, twelve, who had been selling pastries on the sidewalk when he was hit by a bullet in the hip. His father, holding him by the hand, exhaled a deep sigh. His child's suffering was overwhelming him. "Americans should help us, not kill us." He was without rancor, resigned, concentrated in his sadness as a father, stroking his son's hand. My eyes filled with tears; all I could see was this fatherly gesture, this terrible unjust and futile suffering, "collateral damage," the wounding and death of a child. As a war reporter of long standing, I had learned, for survival, not to allow my emotions to take over, and had been obliged to build strong armor around myself. But today, as I surveyed all the pain around me, that armor was riddled with holes.

All of a sudden we heard gunfire outside the hospital. *Peshmerga*, or men claiming to be *peshmerga*, were chasing a looter. When they caught him, they threw him to the ground and pointed a Kalashnikov at his head. Within seconds everyone scattered, fearing a stray bullet.

The most surprising thing was that coalition soldiers were

completely invisible. Where were they? After the disaster in Mosul, they had abandoned the governor's palace, symbolically revealing the power vacuum. Weapons were being provided to everyone as protection. Each party had its own arsenal. The headquarters of the Patriotic Union of Kurdistan in the Kurdish quarter displayed the artillery it had "confiscated" from the collapsed Iraqi army, and offered me an armed escort to travel around the city, an offer I politely declined. To locate Americans, you had to go to the air base — a reflection of the strength and weakness of American soldiers in Iraq. This paradox played a major role in Iraqi disillusionment after the conclusion of initial hostilities. Iraqis had had innumerable fantasies about Americans protecting the Iraqi people, but within the very first days of the war in Mosul, it was clear that there were not enough coalition soldiers on the ground.

This was confirmed to me by Colonel Robert Waltermeyer, commander in chief in Mosul, whom I tracked down at the air base. Welcoming and friendly, he acknowledged his feeling of helplessness. Behind his military discipline, one could sense that he was nonplussed by the extraordinary events he had just gone through. "I would say that Mosul is a unique case, and that we just went through a very unusual week. You have to understand that the last thing we expected was an uprising."

To explain the tragic events that had taken place and the marines' panic, the colonel told the story of the city's capture: "In fact, when we came into Mosul, there were fewer than thirty of us."

How, I asked him, could he have thought they could pacify a city of a couple million inhabitants with thirty men? "The Kurds," he answered, "had put us in contact with one of the tribal chiefs, who guaranteed that everything would work out well."

I had now been in Kurdistan for more than a month, and everyone was urging me to come home: my family of course, but also my editor, René Backmann, who knew from experience that spending too much time rubbing shoulders with danger made you lose your instincts. Besides, like everyone else, I naïvely believed that the war was over, or soon would be.

My driver had found a cassette of the rapper Shaggy in the Irbil market and was playing "It Wasn't Me" nonstop as he drove me to the border. In this extremely prudish country, the incredibly coarse words sounded completely incongruous. While I was glad to be able to listen to something other than Kurdish folk music, I was relieved that my young Muslim driver couldn't speak a word of English.

Then came the post-reporting depression. As usual, I made a list of all the questions I had not been able to cover adequately, starting with the ordeal of the Arabs in the new Kurdistan I had found so moving in Kirkuk. Now that I was in Iran, I rediscovered "peace" and its rules. For the first time in a month, I had to wear my *hijab* again. In Iraq, as in Afghanistan, during the brief time of the war I had been able to move around with my head uncovered. This is what's so intoxicating in wartime — anarchy and the impression of freedom it produces. In the little café in an Iranian village where I was eating, wearing a black veil, behind a tent, I became exasperated and felt like going back to Iraq. A Dutch photographer traveling with me reinforced my regrets with his own. Suppose we tried going back, crossed the border in the opposite direction, while all the other reporters stuck at the gate dreamed only of being able to leave? We knew they would take us for lunatics, but we decided to try.

At the gate, the Iranian customs officer looked at the two of us in disbelief, flabbergasted by our request. Forgetting where I was, I took his hand, which he withdrew with a scandalized snort of laughter — a woman never shakes hands with a man — but it worked: the man had the impression that I was throwing myself at him. He finally granted us an unofficial dispensation for three days, which we knew might cost him dearly. So off we went.

Approaching Irbil from the south, I crossed paths with vans loaded with television sets, mattresses, clothing, and sacks of flour from the oil-for-food program, with whole families perched on top. Kurds and Turkomans were returning to the land from which Saddam had driven them, with the determination of persecuted people finally taking revenge. Entrenched behind front lines, they had never given up hope of rebuilding their villages eradicated by the Baathist regime. It was like a gold rush, all of Kurdistan moving with the mission of chasing Arabs off their property.

My father's family came from Algeria, and I know of the suffering of those who cannot visit the graves of their dead, the sorrow of having personal possessions confiscated, the rancor of people who have been deprived of their sites of memory. I remembered the wound of exile suffered by my Iraqi friend Jabbar, whose mother died when he could not be with her.

I had of course experienced this suffering only by proxy. I had never felt any attachment myself to a patch of earth; I had no family home. For me, the Gordian knot of all battles, the love of the land, was mere intellectual construct. Compassion for attachments formed despite ancestral hatreds did move me. That is why the story of a small Arab farmer, Khamir Muhammad, whom I met in a Kurdish village, touched me. Drawn by the smoke, I walked over and met him in front of the burning houses of his village.

The night before, Khamir told me, Kurds had come into the village of Muntassar brandishing their Kalashnikovs with the brutal arrogance of conquerors and had fired into the straw roofs of the houses. When Khamir's neighbors understood they couldn't hold out any longer against the *peshmerga* who had come to drive them off, some of them set their own houses on fire. Better to lose everything than to see Kurds settle in their houses. But Khamir Muhammad couldn't bring himself to take such a desperate step. "It's my father's house, the house where my children were born. Let them come and kill me here. I'm ready," he told me. Losing his house meant loss of his identity. That morning, Kurdish soldiers had gone so far as to break down his door and hold a Kalashnikov to his throat in front of his four

terrified children. They had even broken the mirror, the only or-
nament in the bare, clean living room of the little house. Squatting on the doorstep, he showed me the bullet holes.

His father had come to the village in 1975, a village of Arab
"colonists" in Kurdish land. "When we got here, there were no
houses. We knew that the land belonged to Kurds and that the
government had confiscated it for us. But what could we do?
Saying no to Saddam meant saying yes to death," said Khamir,
brandishing his identity card, wanting me to know he was born
in 1967 in Tuz, in Kurdistan. He asked me to write down his
name, and asked that I tell him what office he had to go to, since
Saddam had gone. Like so many others who had never had anything to do with reporters, he took me for some kind of official
of the American army come to register his complaints. "Please, I
don't want to be free. I just want to get my land back." His situation seemed so unjust to him, he was convinced that all it would
take was for me to write about him. He was sure that reparation
would be given him. Who could help him? No one, sadly. How
I wish I could have.

That morning, the future Kurdish owner of Khamir's house
had written his name in blue marker on the wall — Barzan, a
name that rang out revenge. Eight thousand men and children
belonging to the Barzani tribe had been arrested one day by the
Iraqi army and never been seen again. Saddam had mentioned
their fate on television, declaring that they were "probably already in hell." Now the Kurds had fought among themselves over
who would have the finest house, the one belonging to the sheikh
of the village. Finally they had written a number on the wall.
"They're going to draw lots for it, like some scrawny chicken,"
Khamir complained.

It was Rambar Rashid, a young Kurd from a neighboring
village, cousin of Barzan, who had pointed out the "Arab" houses
to the *peshmerga* when they had come to "accelerate" the moving. At the time, Rambar sadly explained to me, he hadn't realized the consequences of his action. He now bitterly regretted
having "turned in" his friends. Rambar and Khamir had known

each other since childhood. When they were not separated by trenches and sandbags, they played soccer together, and talked about their plans for the future. "Khamir is my brother," explained Rambar. "Of course, this is Kurdish land, but Saddam forced them to leave their land. The *peshmerga* beat his brother and stole his car. Why do they have to go through all this?" he asked mournfully. That night, to avoid *peshmerga* violence, Khamir would spend the night at Rambar's house, even though their families were at each other's throats.

I was overwhelmed. The time had come for me to tear myself away from this stricken land and go back to my family.

4

The Americans' First Mistakes
August 2003

I N AUGUST 2003 there was still no flight from Amman to Baghdad. Returning to Iraq a few months after the end of the fighting, I had to locate a car to travel the six hundred miles of desert that separated the two capitals. I asked the taxi driver who picked me up at the Amman airport if he knew of a way to get to Baghdad. His answer was to abruptly turn off the highway without warning. After driving five miles in the dark in the middle of nowhere, we finally arrived at a square cement building covered in tiles. A dozen Arabic-speaking men were playing cards next to their large jeeps. There I was, dropped by the taxi driver, alone on the outskirts of Amman with ten thousand dollars in cash in my bag — supposed to last me the next two months in Iraq — wondering how in God's name I would get to my next destination. I had no intention of going in one of those conspicuous cars with tinted windows parked nearby. Looking carefully, I caught sight of a yellow Chevrolet Caprice, a New York taxi that had somehow found its way to Amman. Its owner, Muhammad, was a man of impressive stature, with a crew cut, a short beard, and narrow eyes. I should have known that he would be reluctant to take a woman, fearful of what people would say. He had recently come back from the pilgrimage to Mecca and had a strict sense of propriety, but after much discussion he finally consented to take me. He turned out to be a godsend. This unexpected detour to the outskirts of Amman was to bring me good fortune for the next three years. Muhammad proved to be an intrepid, invaluable partner.

Trained as an engineer, Muhammad, like many out-of-work Iraqis during the last years of sanctions, had out of necessity become a taxi driver. We became inseparable. Whenever I returned to Iraq on a new assignment, he would give up his job, sometimes for months, to accompany me on my adventures. He took countless risks for me, and I came to admire his courage and his determination to improve himself. I adjusted to his fits of temper, and he accepted my deadline jitters and my superstitions. From a driver, he became a genuine colleague, captivated by the adventure of journalism. I remember fondly the moth-eaten stuffed red and yellow frog he kept on his dashboard, which I often stared at for comfort when we found ourselves, as we often did, in dicey situations.

In the course of our long drives over the gravel road, often swept by sandstorms, between Amman and Baghdad, where village streets emerged from dense fog or shimmered in the intense heat like some Arabian wild west, Muhammad and I got to know each other. He had, he claimed, seen Abu Musab al-Zarqawi from a distance in an Amman mosque where he went to pray, and in Saddam's time had driven preachers from al-Zarqawi's group around Baghdad — contacts that would later prove useful. Muhammad was a gentle man, a pacifist who hated violence as much as he hated the American occupation. At first he tried his best to convert me to Islam, but he soon gave up. He enjoyed describing our adventures in epic style in order to persuade Iraqis to confide in me. In a country where formalities of presentation are so important, he often paved the way for me, and I let him go on at length, knowing it was never a waste of time.

We arrived in Baghdad to find the Jordanian embassy in flames, the first of a long series of attacks that were to heat up the summer of 2003. In a city stupefied by heat, only insurgents seemed to be alive. In one spot, smoke spewed from a government office as looters carried off the last of their booty; in another, water pipes exploded before our eyes, transforming the road into a lake into which children swarmed to cool off.

The war was not yet quite over. After its official conclusion, Iraqi companies had patched up hotels in haste to put up reporters and international officials streaming into Baghdad. After ten hours of exhausting travel, I made the rounds of the hotels. That day in Baghdad, the thermometer stood at nearly 140° in the shade. Knowing I would be there for months, it was imperative for me to find suitable accommodations. I sensed that my search for comfort in a city filled with explosions intrigued Muhammad, but he remained as impassive as a statue. I decided on the Hotel al-Hamra. It had an Internet café, and the rooms were like small apartments. It was run by friendly Christians, who greeted me each time I returned with a warm welcome, as though I were coming home.*

My first visit, to the Canal Hotel, was to Ghassan Salame, the UN's number two man in Baghdad, who a few days later barely escaped death in the attack that killed his boss and friend Sergio Vieira de Mello. I remember one of the things that struck me most was the lax security at UN headquarters. During my visit with Salame, I was worried about Muhammad, who had parked just outside; indeed, his car was directly below Vieira de Mello's windows, ten yards from the spot where the bomb-laden truck would explode a few days later. I remember Salame's grief-stricken air when I saw him again as he was about to leave Iraq two days after the attack. He had just made the rounds of the hospitals to visit his severely wounded colleagues. His eyes filled with tears, and he told me that Vieira de Mello, in a last desperate effort to guide rescuers to him, had been able to reach colleagues at the UN mission on his mobile phone a few minutes before his death. "I'm losing blood, the dust is burning my lungs, I'm so thirsty," he had said. The cuffs of his gray pants still contained pieces of concrete from the blast that had killed him.

I saw the site of the attack right after the explosion. An

---

* The hotel has subsequently been blown up.

American soldier was desperately trying to establish his location with his portable GPS device. Another GI was babbling incoherent phrases as though he were dead drunk. The Iraqis, on the other hand, seemed to be delighted, children laughing at the carnage. Then, as the sun set and beautiful orange light streamed through the gravel dust, I became acutely aware of the hostile looks around me. An African American soldier, drenched in sweat and clearly dehydrated, was watching an Iraqi boy slowly drinking mineral water with exaggerated pleasure. The kid offered him the water, the soldier gratefully accepted, and the kid threw him the empty bottle with an air of triumph.

Ghassan Salame, the former Lebanese minister of culture, is a friendly and very intelligent man. He had just met all the influential men in the country, and he was very worried. He drew up a list of the most serious mistakes made by the American administration, about which he was so critical that he forgot to take precautions for himself. He was so involved in acting as intermediary between the various Iraqi parties and factions on the one hand and the occupation forces on the other that he did not recognize that the UN was in grave danger. He spoke on the record, and the American "administrator" Paul Bremer later reprimanded him for having accepted my interview with him.

I found his analysis of the rapidly evolving situation particularly compelling because, even though he had lived through the tragic events of the Lebanese civil war, he was reasonably optimistic about the future of Iraq. At that point in the occupation, he sincerely believed that America could succeed. Lakhdar Brahimi, who became the UN's special envoy to Iraq in 2004, was more pessimistic: he thought that de-Baathification and the dismantling of Saddam's army posed a real risk of civil war. Salame agreed that the American program of de-Baathification might have the most negative consequences for the country: Iraq could not be de-Baathified in the same way Germany had been de-Nazified.

Months before the American invasion, I had interviewed American researchers studying de-Baathification, all of whom concurred it was a crucial matter. The future of the Iraqi nation depended on its success. Who should be kept on to keep the country from disorganization, and who had to be removed to avoid its falling back into some form of dictatorship? The problem would be to find a way to avoid turning the defeat of Saddam into a defeat for the Iraqi people, and particularly for the Sunni portion of the population. It was impossible to find a clear path through the thicket of denunciations and score settling that was sure to spring up after the war. Anyone who had a dispute with his neighbor might accuse him of being a corrupt member of the old regime.

On May 16, 2003, the decree of de-Baathification was issued, arbitrary and blunt like all decrees, penalizing a much larger population than anticipated. It prohibited the holding of public office by heads of regions, branches, sections, and even groups of the Baath Party. Fourteen thousand high school principals and 1,832 university professors suddenly lost their jobs. From one day to the next, they had been transformed from the country's elite into pariahs brooding over the injustice inflicted on them, an army of the educated who had overnight become the war's losers.

The day after my interview with Ghassan Salame, I met Hussain al-Saadi, who had been one of the chief specialists on water pollution in Iraq. Like his colleagues, he had been informed of his dismissal on May 16. His story provided a perfect illustration of the injustice — in fact, folly — of blanket de-Baathification. This distinguished professor, with a degree from an American university, had written more than two hundred articles, many of which had been translated into many languages. He had also supervised thirty-five theses on the subject of pollution. Now he was destitute, a broken man. For twenty-five years, like two million other Iraqis, al-Saadi had been a party member. "To be a professor, you

had to have a Baath Party card," he explained. When he was diag-
nosed with cancer, he tried to leave the party and its long, tedious
meetings, but his request was rejected. The apparatchiks in the
university decided that if he had the strength to teach, he could
continue to do his duty. They even offered him a promotion. "After my request, I was in the hot seat. So, because of my past, I was
strongly advised to become a group leader."

What made him so suspect? I asked, and he told me his
story. In 1978 he coauthored with a European researcher an article on the Shatt al-Arab, an area disputed in the war between
Iran and Iraq. The article spoke of the Arabian Gulf, but in the
final version of the article, which al-Saadi was unable to read, the
European researcher noted in parenthesis that the Arabian Gulf
was another name for the Persian Gulf — wording that, in Saddam's Ubuesque regime during the war with Iran, was a crime
against patriotism punishable by death. Al-Saadi's life was shattered. "The Minister of Education wanted to execute me, even
though I was the editor of the *Journal of the Arabian Gulf.*" In the
end he was merely exiled. He had been scheduled to become
president of Basra University in the south, but instead he was
sent to Irbil in the north, far from his family. "It wasn't my fault,
but I paid for it for the rest of my life." Now he had to expiate another offense of which he considered himself equally guiltless.
He simply could not understand. "All the former Baathists at the
Oil and Electricity Ministries still have their old jobs. So is this
a decree directed against the university?" What saddened him
most, however, was the waste. "They will not be able to replace
me. I am the best specialist on water pollution in Iraq."

Another victim of de-Baathification was Dr. Tarik al-Kubaisy, a
psychiatrist who had been dismissed from Baghdad Hospital. He
agreed to meet me in the small clinic where he now saw patients.
It was located in a bare concrete building in a poor Baghdad
neighborhood still covered with the dust caused by bombs. I
climbed up five flights of stairs and found myself in a shabby

room filled with patients of all ages who had come for treatment because they had been traumatized by the bombing. They were suffocating from the heat as they waited for the doctor. Everyone stared at me, this odd new patient. I wondered how, in this country battered by three wars over the last twenty years, they treated people whom the sound of bombs terrorized. I thought that only rich, cosseted countries took care of the traumatized. Doctor al-Kubaisy, with magnificent blue eyes, had been reluctant to see me. When we met, he could not contain his anger at the Americans. Bitter and aggressive, he railed against his impotence. "Look at us. We're in a desperate state, it's total chaos. Where is good? Where is evil? Who deserves to be kept on? What ridiculous questions!" he fumed. "This morning, one of my colleagues was assassinated in this very building. Three of my neighbors have been burglarized. And my associate had to pay several thousand dollars' ransom to save her children's lives."

As he spoke, we heard gunshots outside the building, an armed attack a few doors away. The doctor didn't seem to notice. The gunfire made me start from my seat, but he didn't even get up from his chair. With all the anxiety, fears, and horrors being uncovered daily, he went on, the entire nation was in need of psychological help. "Our poor, traumatized country has fewer than a hundred psychiatrists. Half of them are army officers or Baathists. Do you think this is the time to dismiss them?" According to al-Kubaisy, speaking as a psychiatrist, under the dictatorship everyone suffered. And the Baathists were even more traumatized than the others by their feeling of powerlessness and frustration: "Do you think we had any choice? We either had to leave the country and subject our families to reprisals or keep quiet and smooth things over." The doctor told me that he usually did his best to act as a buffer between idiotic orders from Saddam's inner circle and the students, for example, when they were "summoned" to rallies in the midst of exams. Once, the psychiatrist had flatly refused to obey an order. "We were supposed to cut off the ears of all the deserters from the war against

Iran. I refused in spite of all the threats, and our hospital did not have to comply." According to him, what Iraq needed now was not to find scapegoats but rather to promote national reconciliation, particularly because he was far from certain that democracy would triumph through this new distribution of jobs. "Shiite religious extremists are gradually replacing the dismissed professors, for example in Mustansiriye University."

I decided to pay a visit to the venerable Baghdad university and hear the students' version of events. Saad, a Shiite fourth-year student in history, who had come looking for his exam results, told me he was happy that the Baathists had been dismissed from the university. He had even gone to Muqtada al-Sadr, the extremist leader of the Shiite community in Baghdad, and denounced some professors who favored resistance to the American occupation. The rather distasteful delight Saad seemed to be taking in plotting revenge was revealing of the score-settling that had gone on in the university. Saad acknowledged that he, like virtually all the students, had been a member of the Baath Party, reminding me they had no choice but to join: the party card opened the way to scholarships and good grades.

A group of students of English literature, made up of two Shiites and two Sunnis, explained to me: "No professor could be appointed to a senior position unless he belonged to the Baath Party." According to these students, the Baathist professors had tried to help students. Only a small number of them had written reports to curry favor with the party hierarchy. Amar, one of the students, had been the subject of one of these reports, placing him under a cloud throughout his studies and effectively isolating him from his fellow students. He nevertheless found the dismissal of his professors unjust. "We don't understand the Americans' methods. It would have been very easy to question the students. With our eyes closed, we would have been able to identify the ones who had ruined our lives from the ones who had protected us."

As I traveled throughout the country, I got a sense of the

growing anger against the occupation forces. It would have been so easy to mobilize intellectuals for the construction of the new Iraq. Instead, so many had been made potential enemies.

A few days later I decided to go to Baquba, a city between Baghdad and the Iranian border that was soon to become a frequent target of attacks. I had been told that the former heads of Saddam's dreaded secret service, the Mukhabarat, were going to stage a demonstration there as a sign of their dissatisfaction. Only in Iraq could such paradoxes be found. The demonstration was an ultimatum from Saddam's henchmen to the Americans: either the occupation forces guaranteed them a job with pay, or they would join the resistance. The ball was in the Americans' court, and, according to UN officials Ghassan Salame and Lakhdar Brahimi, their failure to respond quickly was the coalition's second serious mistake.

This is how the confrontation took place. When I got to Baquba at nine in the morning, two black American army helicopters were skimming over the rooftops. At the checkpoint on the way into the city, a plump little boy leaned into the window of my car. "If you have any weapons, you better turn back. I think they're looking for poor Saddam," he whispered to Muhammad. Humvees, jeeps, and tanks patrolled the streets. Soldiers were on a war footing, nervously fingering their weapons and sweating out of fear and from the 120° heat. They too had been told of the dreaded Mukhabarat demonstration. The Americans had been negotiating under pressure for two months with these henchmen of the former regime, suspected of being behind a large number of the attacks that had recently bloodied Baquba. To persuade them not to demonstrate, the coalition forces had promised to pay them by August 24, but forty Mukhabarat leaders, ignoring the promise, had assembled in front of coalition headquarters to keep up the pressure. I stared in fascination at the members of the most hated institution of Saddam's regime, the pinnacle of arbitrary rule, a collection of angry men, all looking like brothers, with identical mustaches. Until then, the secret police had been hiding in their houses both to avoid reprisals from the population that hated them and to avoid being arrested by the Americans. It was fascinating to see them like a little army, walking around in the open in Baquba, the city of orange groves and orchards. What surprised me most was to see that passersby paid them barely any heed, much less wanted to assault them. I realized that after more than three months of American occupation, the local population had almost come to sympathize with the unemployed secret agents who had become like everyone else: fathers who could no longer feed their children. It seemed unbelievable that even these dreaded and dreadful characters assumed they had rights, like ordinary public officials, asking to be paid. The fact that American soldiers looked on them as the SS of Iraq apparently didn't faze them in the least.

The chaos made it impossible for me to photograph them or even to get their names. The atmosphere was electric.

"If they don't pay us, we're prepared to kill all the Americans," said Smaïn, thirty-five, clearly the organizer of the demonstration and the "intellectual" of the group. "When we're sure that they refuse to pay our salaries and hire us again, we'll drive them crazy. In Diyala Province, all our men are ready for battle," he explained.

Karim, a captain in the Mukhabarat who had shot himself twice in the leg so he could take a retirement denied by his superiors, went further: "We know exactly how to strike where it hurts the most. That's our job. Any private American company that moved in here would be making a big mistake."

By August 2003 the threat was specific, and it continued to shadow reconstruction. For the Americans, the danger in this city of 250,000, located less than sixty miles from the Iranian border, emanated from Tehran. In June, they had driven out militants of the Supreme Council of the Islamic Revolution in Iraq, the chief Shiite political power in the country, which was closely tied to Iran. Taking advantage of the power vacuum, this party had taken over the mayor's office and hung pictures of Khomeini

on the walls, while their armed militia, the Badr Brigade, policed
the city streets. But now, for American soldiers who didn't know
which way to turn, the face of the enemy had changed. Watching
them shifting around nervously, I had the sense that they felt besieged by demons in Baquba.

During the demonstration, Hussein, a Shiite jurist who had
agreed to be my guide in Baquba, recognized one of the former
secret service officers, whose name was Abu Ibrahim. To my surprise, he fell into the arms of this man, who apparently had offered him a helping hand at a time when he was being harassed
by Saddam's security apparatus: a passport, a bank deposit returned, little things that could mean the difference between life
and death under the old regime. Intrigued, I asked Hussein if I
could interview Abu Ibrahim, and after a good deal of hesitation,
the man agreed to see me in his home, provided I took no notes
during the conversation.

I sat on a brown ottoman in the living room of his house,
which was made of concrete. Paintings showing him in uniform
against an emerald green background decorated the small room.
A woman's hands slid a tray into the room: even when veiled,
women are reluctant to appear in front of strangers. While
speaking to me, Abu Ibrahim nervously fingered the fabric of his
dishdasha, the traditional white tunic. In the chaos of postwar
Iraq, he knew he was at the mercy of denunciations that continued to pour into American headquarters. As they were translated
to me, I memorized his words, fearful of forgetting details.

Abu Ibrahim acknowledged that he had cried when the statues of Saddam were toppled. While most Iraqis claimed to detest
the former dictator as much as the Americans, the secret service
agent had no such qualms. The day he saw Saddam in an official
procession in Baquba in 1988 was the greatest day in his life, he
told me. "His face exalted you, made you feel better. He was a god
for his people." Abu Ibrahim showed me photographs of the former president, stashed away as though they were precious. The
image of Abd al-Karim Qasim, the general who had overthrown
the Hashemite monarchy, was engraved on the lid of a teakettle.

Abu Ibrahim, who had at first claimed to have nothing in common with the demonstrators, acknowledged that the secret service agents had asked him to be their spokesman. He had refused, because he knew that during this anarchic time it was impossible to please everyone. "We have moved from silence into cacophony," as he cleverly summed it up.

During the war with the Americans, in spite of the bombs dropped by the B-52s, he had been the last to leave Mukhabarat headquarters. With his hand on his heart, he swore he had never tortured anyone, nor had he ever written one of those reports that ensured a promotion for the author and the most terrible punishment for the subject. But he admitted that he was not a choirboy. When I asked him whether he had killed anyone, he laughed and answered: "War was my whole life. I was also a lieutenant in the artillery; you can draw your own conclusion." He had killed on the Iranian border and in Kuwait. Oddly, the only place in which he had no blood on his hands was Kurdistan. "I went to Halabja with Saddam's cousin, Ali Hassan al-Majid, 'Chemical Ali,' but the *peshmerga* took me prisoner at the very beginning," he said with a smile. I asked him whether he would have participated in the gassing of tens of thousands of Kurds if he had not been taken prisoner. He looked at me coldly with his green eyes. "I am a soldier. I obey orders." Now Abu Ibrahim, along with his comrades, was asking the occupation forces for pay and a job. "The secret service, like the police, is part of the essential machinery of the state."

As I listened to this man, I understood that if the coalition forces did not reintegrate these officials whose profession had been to ruin the lives of Iraqis, and who only wanted to serve a new master, they would face difficulty in the days ahead.

5

The Ominous Shadow of Ali
August 2003

O N AUGUST 28, after several fruitless trips to the Shiite holy city of Najaf, I was told that Ayatollah Mohammed Baqir al-Hakim, one of the most important figures in the Shiite community, considered a possible future president of Iraq, had agreed to my request for an interview. As I waited for an audience in his Koranic school, oppressed by the heat, my long black *abaya* kept falling open before the reproachful looks of the faithful. I hadn't yet mastered the skill of keeping the synthetic material from slipping off my head. Straightening it out, I gulped in the steaming air between the two strips of cloth around my mouth. How in this tropical heat did Iraqi women tolerate their costume? It was pure torment. I silently cursed this impossible garb, cursing men in general.

For the moment, in the murky, sweltering heat brought on by a power cut — a normal occurrence in life in Iraq — the clanking of weapons and the buzzing of metal detectors punctuated the monotonous rhythm of the prayers, a mixture of sounds I could never get used to. The ayatollah told me that he felt threatened. A few days earlier, an assassination attempt against his nephew had killed his three bodyguards. He knew he was a prime target for those who wanted to destabilize the country, primarily because he was a respected figure. In a community in which legitimacy was earned by burying one's martyrs, Ayatollah al-Hakim had paid a heavy price: 29 of the 125 members of his family arrested by Saddam had been assassinated, and 18 others had disappeared. Also a target because he was more "moderate" than others, he had urged the Shiites to "exhaust all peaceful methods" to bring American occupation to an end. He had invoked the example of the Prophet, who had attempted to convert the unbelievers in Mecca for thirteen long years before launching the jihad. It was perhaps because he was speaking to a woman that he assumed a condescending tone, but in any case I found him rather unpleasant. His sayyid's black turban emphasized the pallor of his face, and his severe gaze contrasted with his delicate features. After twenty-three years of exile in Iran, the ayatollah had reached the end of his patience, like other powerful Shiite figures whose quietism, piety, and patience concealed formidable political ambitions. His elusive smile was not the smile of a modest man. In fact, he flatly told me that a good deal of the political normalization the United States was calling for depended directly on him. He seemed to have thought of everything. I could see that it was probably out of self-interest rather than to follow the *ishtihad*, the exegesis of the sacred texts, that he had stood back from temporal matters, following the example of the great quietist *marjas*, like Khomeini before he had come to power.

That evening, August 28, while worshippers were reciting the somber chants commemorating the martyrdom of Hussein, the son of Ali, who had been assassinated along with his seventy-two companions by the Umayyads, the ayatollah withdrew into the small office next to the prayer hall to prepare the next day's sermon, which he invited me to attend. The prospect was tempting, as it was a rare opportunity for a woman, but I had to decline because I had a deadline to meet. Muhammad and I left. This turned out to be providential for Muhammad and me. A few minutes after delivering a sermon denouncing the coalition forces for their inability to guarantee his safety, Ayatollah al-Hakim was blown to pieces by a car bomb that killed eighty-two and wounded nearly two hundred. Despite painstaking efforts by the employees of the morgue, who attempted to assemble the shattered body parts on a stretcher, they were able to find only one of his hands, his pen, his watch, and his black turban.

*   *   *

I returned to Najaf from Baghdad to attend the funeral of Ayatollah Mohammed Baqir al-Hakim, a melancholy practice I was
getting used to more and more in Iraq. Dozens of famous and
unknown Iraqis whom I had met or interviewed in the course of
my stay had later been assassinated, which both depressed me
and left me with the gnawing feeling that I was bringing misfortune to others while being spared myself.

Before I left, several other reporters warned me to be careful: apparently mines had been laid all over the road from Baghdad to Najaf. In Iraq, I was learning, there was no way to
distinguish between rumor and truth. My usual translator, a
Sunni named Mazen, refused to go to Najaf with me. His wife
had begged him not to go, worried that the Shiite crowd in
mourning would boil over. His fear was indicative of the problems that stemmed from the coexistence of religious groups in
Iraq. I ended up traveling to the holy city with Muhammad and
Hussein, a Shiite translator.

The day after the attack, tens of thousands of men and
women, tightly pressed together, streamed through the narrow
lanes leading to the mausoleum of Ali in Najaf. The atmosphere
was oppressive. Along with Muhammad — and as usual uncomfortable in my black *abaya* — I found myself engulfed in the midst
of the crowd.

Suddenly a car plowed through our group and drove up to
the small mosque next to the house inhabited by Khomeini during his exile in Najaf from 1965 to 1978. The car belonged to
Abdel Aziz, Ayatollah al-Hakim's brother. When he appeared,
laments and tears intensified. "How could you accept, Imam Ali,
the death of Mohammed Baqir at your threshold?" cried the
men, beating their chests. This worship of martyrs and devotion
to contrition was far from the Sunni world with which I was familiar.

It is always difficult to predict the reactions of a crowd, but I
quickly sensed that this mass of Shiites was not well disposed
toward the very foreigners who had liberated them from Saddam's

yoke. "Bush, Bin Laden, Tony Blair, all war criminals," some of them growled, looking at me and my fellow reporters. A small group of men shook their fists at me, and one of them challenged: "And what have *you* done for us?" at which point I realized that my *abaya* had slipped and I was no longer invisible in the middle of the crowd. They wanted to know my nationality, but I knew that being French would win me no friends, because in the Shiite community the French are hated almost as much as the Americans. "You French are no better than the Americans. You and al-Jazeera spread nothing but lies. You supported Saddam." And a dozen furious men pushed me out of the procession. Muhammad explained that we had been with the assassinated martyr the day before. But far from calming them down, this information intensified their fury. They stared at me as though they thought I had been responsible for the death of their leader. I felt threatened . . . and scared.

I knew Iraqis needed to finger the guilty, and to pinpoint scapegoats responsible for their misfortunes. This habit of accusing others was also a way of clearing their name of any crimes they might be suspected of. The Shiite community of Iraq was itself divided into many conflicting factions, which created daily inner conflicts.

Off to one side, the police were arresting men who looked like Wahhabis. The crowd rumbled, and the atmosphere grew threatening. I sensed that things might soon turn even more ugly. Riots are much more frightening than war itself and, as I had already experienced, in this country they were often more deadly. Today I heard the same refrain everywhere: "The American occupation is responsible for the bloodshed. This is anarchy. The borders are porous. The occupation forces have permitted the deadly alliance between the Wahhabis and the forces of the old regime." It was eminently clear that it would take all the charisma of the spiritual guides of the holy city to prevent the Shiite mob from taking arms against the invader.

*   *   *

Lost in the middle of the dense crowd flowing like a human river through all the lanes leading to the golden dome, I recalled my earlier visits to Najaf. A few weeks before, I had come to see an Iraqi poet friend, Jabbar, who had returned to his native city with his French wife and a group of friends. The enthusiasm of his French friends was touching; in this country just "liberated" from Saddam's yoke, they had decided to set up a humanitarian organization. Under the spell of Jabbar's charisma, we traveled around the city lulled by poetic tales of his bookish childhood. His sweet memories of the enchanted landscapes of his youth placed a screen between us and today's harsh reality. At that point, we had seen few signs of rising Shiite fundamentalism. Even the dark narrow alley leading to the extremist leader Muqtada al-Sadr's office had had an almost welcoming air, and we had barely noticed the beggar rolling around on the ground outside the teeming courtyard from which an ancient bearded cleric dressed in black had issued to drive me away without looking at me because I was a woman. Of course, because it was my job, I had in fact detected the threatening clouds gathering in the darkening sky, but I didn't want to burden the dreams of these Frenchmen with stories of my reporting from all parts of the country. They had stars in their eyes, and they dismissed the pessimism I expressed like an irritable prophet of doom. "You reporters are always obsessed with trains that don't run on time." For her visit, Jabbar's wife had put on veils decorated with sequins, light-years from the dress of the sequestered women of Najaf, always in mourning. She had arrived in the imagined Mesopotamia of her poet.

A week later I returned to Najaf with another reporter, a special correspondent for a conservative French newspaper. When he saw me put on my "sock" (my underveil) and my *abaya* as we got close to the city, he looked at me in dismay. "To think that that's what's in store for Frenchwomen," he sighed. His reaction was the same as that of a Moroccan friend when she had seen me put on a chador in the streets of Sanaa in Yemen, frowning at what she perceived as my acquiescing in the face of Islamic fanaticism. I actually took pleasure in being invisible in a country where everyone stares at strangers, and had fun disguising myself. Wearing the veil had much less weight for me than for her, since she had more than once faced the contempt of her fellow citizens for not wearing it. But in Iraq, the people I had gone to interview would simply not have seen me had I not been veiled. And wearing the veil was not something that could be taken lightly. You only needed to wear an *abaya* in Iraq or a burqa in Afghanistan for a few hours to realize the extent to which it signified the submission of women to the rule of men rather than the rule of God.

My French colleague Bertrand and I had come to Najaf to report on the executions of Baathists that had been taking place in secret within tribal groups. We first went to see the family of one of the prominent men in the city who had been assassinated. The house was easy to locate from the crowd of men all dressed in black milling about in front of it. They offered to share their funeral meal with us, during which they related the circumstances of the murder, in which, as was often the case, economic motives (a dispute about a piece of land) were grafted onto political motives. The family and other people in the neighborhood identified the guilty man, a religious sheikh, head of one of the most powerful tribes in the city.

After paying our respects, we left for the sheikh's house, wondering what pretext we could use to approach him. We obviously couldn't start by asking him about the murder of his neighbor. After an hour of convoluted discussion about the current political situation in Iraq, I decided to jump in. "Your neighbor says that you killed his son because you wanted to get your hands on his land and that you accused him of being a Baathist. What do you think about the growing number of revenge killings in Najaf?"

Neither my translator, a former general in Saddam's army, nor Bertrand's, a former colonel, wanted to translate my question. They politely deferred to each other:

"You have a higher rank, General, the honor should be yours."

"I will do nothing of the kind, Colonel. Please, you ask the question. That's an order."

The sheikh looked on, mystified, as the two men deferred to each another, both terrified. One of them finally made up his mind. He took about ten minutes to translate the question, it seemed, as diplomatically as possible, but it did no good. At the mention of his neighbors, the sheikh exploded.

Bertrand, a man who tended to wear his feelings on his sleeve, rolled his eyes and turned to me with a look that said, We'd better beat a fast retreat! The scene between Saddam's former soldiers, the fury of the sheikh, and Bertrand's facial expressions made me think I was witnessing an Iraqi vaudeville show, and I burst out laughing. Meanwhile, the increasingly furious sheikh turned to the translator, demanding an explanation for the hysterical laughter that had reduced me to tears. For a long time I couldn't get a grip on myself. As I asked another question, I burst out laughing again. The more frightened my companions grew, the more I laughed. I was no longer listening, only seeing the grimacing faces of this commedia dell'arte.

Outside, the sheikh's security guards armed with Kalashnikovs were making noise. Even the sound of their voices was not enough to calm me down, and I was still shaking with laughter like a fool when I took my leave. Only much later, on the road to Baghdad, did I manage to calm down. Only then did I realize that my laughter stemmed essentially from my near hysteria . . . and that it could well have cost me my life.

6

The DHL Attack, Before and After
November 2003

O N SATURDAY, NOVEMBER 22, 2003, a plane chartered by the DHL delivery service company was hit by a surface-to-air missile, the first attack of its kind in Iraq. Although one wing caught fire, in an extraordinary feat of flying the pilots managed to land the aircraft relying entirely on manipulation of the engines.

A few days earlier, through a trusted contact, I had been seated in the small garden of a house in the center of Baghdad, across from the man who was to carry out the attack, Abu Abdullah. Given who he was, I listened to what he had to say with a fair amount of suspicion. Nonetheless, at that time it was very difficult to make contact with insurgent forces. A few reporters had managed to get interviews with masked fighters claiming membership, but almost none had seen them face to face, much less in action. Before meeting with Abu Abdullah, I had met at least two fake "fighters" whose stories I did not believe. In the shady underworld of Baghdad, swarming as it was with informers, spies, and former Baathists trying to earn a living, it was tricky to tell truth from falsehood. And so I couldn't help wondering whether this no longer youthful Iraqi was indeed the merciless fighter he claimed to be.

Abu Abdullah — his nom de guerre — was a man of about fifty, with a tired smile. His double chin covered with a pepper-and-salt stubble did not exactly make him look warlike. There

were "about a hundred" in his "combat cell," he said, which had
no name. Since the "resistance" had begun, he assured me, he
had killed American soldiers almost every week. Regarding his
soft face and stooped posture, I reserved judgment. I asked him
to tell me about the last action he had taken part in. He ticked off
two: a mortar recently fired at Paul Bremer's headquarters in the
Green Zone and blowing up an Iraqi army truck on the road to
Mahmudia the day before our meeting. Abu Abdullah claimed to
be in charge of logistics for the group's "operations." When he
was not carrying grenade launchers from one resistance group to
another around Baghdad, he was looking for bomb-making information on the Internet for his engineers, trafficking detonators, and bringing weapons for repair to former members of the
Iraqi artillery.

As he described his feats of arms, I recalled images of massacres that had taken place during the first days of Ramadan:
bodies decapitated by shell fragments, children covered in blood.
After those terrible days, the natural support of the Iraqi population for the "resistance" had dried up, suggesting that they were
for the first time making a distinction between resistance to the
occupation and terrorism. What made an enemy combatant into
a terrorist? When I met Abu Abdullah, it was still possible to believe that the deaths of children and other civilians were "collateral damage" of the war. Members of the "resistance" like Abu
Abdullah disavowed those crimes rather than excusing them, as
al-Zarqawi's group would later do. But American intervention
had also caused the death of children and civilians. Was everything just a matter of viewpoint? This was the question I never
stopped asking throughout the war.

The question now put to Abu Abdullah was how he justified
the death of Iraqi children. In fact, Abu Abdullah, who defined
himself as a Muslim fighter dedicated to fighting in the name of
religion to liberate his people from the "invader," condemned
these attacks against the "innocent." He claimed to hate Saddam
as much as the foreign fighters who were interfering in their national struggle. "Why is everybody trying to steal our liberation

from us?" he demanded indignantly. "Our group strongly condemns the actions in which Iraqi civilians are killed; the people who carried them out are trying to discredit the Islamic resistance." He also condemned suicide attacks, which he said were funded by "foreigners" and carried out by destitute men who paid with their lives for the financial security of their families. "Sometimes they're offered as much as twenty thousand dollars for their families. They have nothing, so they sacrifice themselves. They carry out one attack, when they could have carried out a hundred. From the point of view of the struggle," he concluded, "it's a total waste."

Wary at first, Abu Abdullah eventually confided in me quite openly. Like all Iraqis who had been silent for so long, he felt the need to talk, to complain, to justify his combat, which for him was simply "a struggle for colonial emancipation like all the others in the world" — language very different from that of the Zarqawi group I met later, who explained with fanatical logic that the "innocent" who perished in their attacks were blessed to have been "chosen" to die, for God would take them to paradise and would treat them with the favor reserved for martyrs.

Abu Abdullah went on to explain that he was an entrepreneur who, to make ends meet, sometimes carried out small contracts for Americans. He loved France and had been there several times. In fact, his father had a doctorate in economics from the Sorbonne. "My father was very nationalistic and very religious, and this education inspires my combat today."

When did he decide to take up clandestine action against the "occupier"? I asked.

He told me about a day in May when an American soldier wanted to check his car's registration papers. "I didn't have them. He confiscated my car, and lifted my arm behind my back until he broke it." Abu Abdullah got up from his chair. He acted out the soldier's movements and relived the pain and humiliation. It was at that moment, he said, that he had decided to join the "resistance." Even though he hated Saddam, "a tyrant and a bad Muslim," he had decided to contact some Baathists who, he thought, would be eager to go after the "invader," to no avail. "Cowards, who were still stunned by American bombs," said the mujahid. It had taken months before, frustrated at not being reincorporated into the army, generals and lieutenants decided to join them. "They came," he said, "only when American vulnerability on the ground was blindingly obvious."

His account reminded me of the demonstrations I had witnessed in August 2003, when members of Saddam's secret services were demanding to be paid. What would have happened if they had been rehired then? Would guerrilla fighting have been so fierce? Would those extremely nationalistic men have allowed "foreign fighters" to invade Iraqi soil?

That day, Abu Abdullah acknowledged to me that, with the help of former officers in Saddam's army, the insurgent forces had entered a new stage. "We are bigger and better organized, and we now use remote detonators for our bombs. We also have a large number of Strela surface-to-air missiles we plan to use against American helicopters and aircraft."

In the course of the months I had spent in Iraq, I had seen the unformed resistance of the beginning take on shape and substance. Since the Americans had declared a state of maximum alert, Abu Abdullah had merely scouted locations. "We are not attacking; we're waiting. They always end up letting down their guard."

How could I be sure he was telling the truth, that he was indeed who he said he was? After several hours of discussions, Abu Abdullah agreed to introduce my driver and guide Muhammad and me to the ten-man cell preparing the next attack near Mahmudia. They did not yet know that their target would be the DHL plane. No one else would be able to come with us, especially not my current translator, a Shiite who was later taken hostage, together with my colleague Florence Aubenas, from the daily paper *Libération*, and held for five months. Before setting out, Abu Abdullah had to inform his third and youngest wife of his absence. She finally came out onto the porch, dressed entirely in black, wearing gloves, her face covered by a black veil. She had a long discussion with her husband, which sounded like an argument. "My wife is very jealous," he apologized, pointing at me. The only thing missing was a rolling pin. Even guerrilla fighters have marital problems — this man had thirteen children!

Off we went with Abu Abdullah, and before long we were driving down a road bordered by scattered farms, somewhere between Yusufiya and Mahmudia southwest of the Iraqi capital. We came upon women in multicolored clothing carrying bundles of plump sweet dates on their shoulders. Fall had already begun to yellow the leaves on the trees. As we left the highway leading to Karbala and then to Kuwait, the air became full of the perfume of flowers.

Although I was far from the tumult of Baghdad, the presence of war could be felt, even here. In tanks and Humvees, American soldiers, eyes peeled, fingers on the triggers, pointed their automatic weapons at anything that moved. No one dared to go down side roads. The countryside was under constant surveillance. Pointing to a path snaking through a palm grove and along a cornfield, Abu Abdullah explained that coalition forces now referred to it as Death Alley because so many men had been lost there.

The farther we drove, the more Abu Abdullah kept getting lost, which was not exactly reassuring. At one point, when we turned back in the midst of a labyrinth of dirt roads, I grew impatient, wondering if he really was the fighter he claimed to be. A warrior who couldn't find his weapons cache? If he didn't bring me to his group and their arsenal, I would have no proof that what he had said was true. Finally we drove up to a large cement farmhouse, which Abu Abdullah identified as headquarters for the military arm of his cell.

Ahmed, aged twenty-three, the younger brother of the owner, invited his "brother in arms" into the small prayer room. A few months earlier, the American army had thrown Ahmed and his three brothers in jail because one of his neighbors had "turned him in" for a $600 reward. The coalition forces had found twenty-one bombs and the same number of grenade launchers in the farmhouse. Since that time, weapons had been buried in a safe place some distance away. The four boys had been released after promising to cooperate with the American army. On this farm, the one person hated as much as the Americans was Saddam. In 1996 one of Ahmed's uncles, a member of the Republican Guard, had tried to foment a coup d'état against the president. His entire family ended up in the dictator's jails, and upon their release Saddam confiscated all their property. Yet at this time the Americans were claiming that everyone fighting against the occupation was a supporter of the former dictator.

Ahmed, who had been married the month before, had never spent more than a few hours with his wife. "My country needs me," the young man explained. Among the guerrilla forces, Ahmed had received intensive training in the firing of the Russian Strela surface-to-air missile, a light maneuverable weapon fired from the shoulder like a bazooka. That day, at their invitation, I was to attend the final rehearsal, and in a few days Ahmed would fire at American targets. He proudly displayed his SAM-14, detailing its technical characteristics. His friend Sardar, a Kurd who had specialized in this missile in Saddam's army, was training him in the delicate handling of the sophisticated weapon. According to the little group, the coalition was offering $3,000 to anyone who turned one of these missiles in.

I asked Abu Abdullah how he had met his comrades in Yusufiya.

"I would often stop at the nearest mosque for evening prayer," he said. "When we came out we would talk. You would keep your peace in the presence of people who sympathized with the Americans, but it didn't take very long to find people who shared our ideas," he explained.

For security reasons, Abu Abdullah knew only the pseudonyms of the other mujahideen, and yet he claimed that he "loved them more than [his] own children." Cells formed and dissolved as circumstances required, depending on planned attacks. There was no cooperation between them. In fact, the mujahideen did not seem to be very well organized. "Sometimes, several of us turn up at the same target, or else we discover when we're organizing an operation that some of our friends have already been there before us." Was it these amateurs the American army was depicting as the devil assailing troops? Like his companions, Abu Abdullah certainly exaggerated the number of his victims and often described attacks that were never reported by the coalition forces. The insurgents were all living in a paranoid world, deluding themselves with the wildest rumors about the number of American deserters who had traded their combat fatigues for dishdashas and disappeared into the Iraqi desert.

While they were talking to me so candidly in this concrete house, the small group of men were playing with the numerous weapons literally lying around. Ahmed brandished his Kalashnikov like a kid. Then he grabbed his antitank grenade launcher, screwed on the thruster, and stroked the aluminum safety catch that kept him from firing the grenade from this RPG-7. An hour earlier, I had doubted I was with "real insurgents." I now felt uncomfortable, lost in the Iraqi countryside in the middle of this arsenal. Ahmed laughed and pointed the weapon directly at me to frighten me, playing the usual macho game. My predictable reaction was to show my fear; then I realized I was falling into their cliché of a fragile woman.

From the time I had arrived, they kept badgering me with questions: What I was doing there instead of being home with my husband and my daughter? My very presence was clear evidence of how degenerate the West was, which allowed its women to go off to cover war situations! When I responded that sometimes Western women go on missions abroad while their husbands stay home and take care of the children, they doubled up with laughter. The timid women preparing a meal in the kitchen barely dared speak to me; they giggled, hiding their faces in their hands. Their attitude, emanating from centuries of inherited servitude, had become second nature.

One thing the mujahideen loved as much as weapons was the media. Hassan was their film man. On the small screen of his

Sony camera, he showed the "rushes" of the latest attacks: a booby-trapped Humvee, another American army vehicle in flames, grenades fired at a tank — the everyday life of American troops and the men fighting against them.

Suddenly faces became expressionless. Silently the men picked up their weapons. The time had come for the attack. The ones left behind looked serious; they blessed the "fighters" and asked me if I was sure I wanted to go with them. In my heart of hearts I wasn't sure, but I hadn't come this far to stop here.

After a quarter hour zigzagging on dirt tracks on the edge of tomato and corn fields in a battered pickup truck, the little group stopped in the open country, pulled out their binoculars, observed planes flying overhead, and checked their missiles. A few yards away, farm women were tying up their bundles of dates and wringing out their *abayas* the streams had soaked, completely indifferent to and oblivious of these heavily armed men tramping through their fields. I moved off, about three-quarters of a mile away from them. Half an hour later they rejoined me in a state of deep distress — the SAM-14 had jammed. They then offered to give me a guided tour of the arms caches on the farm. Every small farmhouse had a buried arsenal. In one spot, next to a field of yellow squash, a farmer dug up and showed me helicopter missiles that had been modified so they could be used from the ground. In another cache were rocket launchers, grenades, and dozens of boxes of Kalashnikov bullets. In still another were artillery shells.

The most incredible thing to me was that virtually since the beginning of the insurgency Abu Abdullah's group had been stocked. Not once had it bought any weapons: all of them had been picked up by Iraqi peasants when the army disintegrated, to be exchanged or to be used. As for the TNT with which they filled their remotely detonated bombs, it was so easy to find that the group didn't even bother to keep a supply of it. A dozen or so miles from the farm was one of the largest explosives factories in the Middle East, the al-Qaaqa factory, an industrial complex more than twenty miles in length. According to the IAEA, more than 350 tons of explosives had disappeared from this factory, a disappearance that hit the headlines when John Kerry made it an issue in the 2004 presidential elections. In any event, in November 2003 it was still possible to take whatever you wanted from the gigantic hangars covered with earth — which is precisely what Abu Abdullah's group had done. Thanks to the precious red powder, his companions assured me, they had blown up a convoy on the road between Asua and the Basra highway a few days before our meeting.

I asked them to show me the factory. Muhammad and I followed the pickup truck down the road to the factory. We were driving slowly, too slowly. An American patrol intercepted us, surrounded our vehicles, and had the passengers get out in pairs. With my veil on my head, the soldiers took me for an Iraqi. I was scared stiff, and I was sure they could hear my heart beating. A young female soldier on a tank pointed her automatic weapon at us. Abu Abdullah, who had gotten out of the truck smiling, joked in Arabic with the American officer of Jordanian origin who was questioning him. At that time, relations between Americans and Iraqis could still sometimes be cordial. After a few minutes, they let us go on.

When we got to the factory, no one blocked our access. The few armed Iraqi guards we encountered didn't even ask us what we were doing there. The spectacle was fascinating: as you walked through this city of bombs, artillery shells, and explosives, you knew you were in insurgents' paradise. The entire military history of Iraq was spread out before you. When the regime fell, many looters had blown themselves up fighting over the shells littering the ground. In truth, it would have taken an entire army to guard the site. The unimaginable reality was that this arsenal was free for all to help themselves! I was surprised but not stunned. Everything in Iraq was so unbelievable that one's senses soon became dulled. There I was, alone in this factory, which for unexplained reasons didn't seem to be of interest to anyone, neither the press nor the American army. It seemed inconceivable that no one stopped the looting of dangerous weapons! I began to have doubts about myself, my vision, my surprise, and the importance of what I was seeing. It wasn't until the time of the American election that I thought again about my visit to the al-Qaaqa factory.

The next day, an American reporter friend asked me to go with her to a farewell party being given in the Green Zone by a CIA agent she knew. How ironic, I thought, after what I had just seen, to find myself on the other side of the war — and, what was more, in one of its secret corners. By attending the party, I hoped I might find out more about the al-Qaaqa factory.

We walked fast in the darkness in the Green Zone, a nightly target for mortars. The camp housed both civilians and soldiers, a little piece of America. John, who was leaving after six months in Iraq, solemnly handed out small farewell gifts — a cap and a T-shirt to a fifty-five-year-old Iraqi whose two sons had risked their lives by infiltrating terrorist groups. There was good music, and I started dancing to a reggae beat with a federal agent, who turned out to be an excellent dancer. If you forgot the setting, dancing a few minutes in a carefree spirit, you could imagine you were at a party in the United States. In speaking to federal agents that night, I realized they hadn't seen much of the country. At the time, these men were still sure of the success of their mission in Iraq. They carried with them their world, their self-assurance, their perfect organization that proved completely incompatible with the Iraqi world.

A veteran of the Vietnam War, responsible for demining operations, told me of his concern about the stream of explosives and fragmentation bombs flowing so freely through the country: "I have only one fear, and that is that we'll end up telling the Iraqis to manage on their own now that Saddam is no longer in power. That would be a catastrophe."

I thought of my recent immersion with the insurgents, of the gigantic explosives supermarket of al-Qaaqa, and wondered what he would think if I told him he had no idea of how much weaponry was available to all comers. Later I was introduced to one of the generals responsible for training the new Iraqi army, and I decided I should tell him briefly what I had seen, assuming he might have the authority to do something about it. I asked him point-blank why al-Qaaqa was no longer guarded, and I could see he had no idea what I was talking about. It turned out he had just arrived and had never heard of what had once been the largest explosives factory in the Middle East. I realized he wasn't really listening to me, merely making small talk while he sipped his whiskey, obviously eager to think about something else.

The day of the DHL attack, Abu Abdullah, its perpetrator, was in a car waiting for me outside my hotel. The bomb thrower of Yusufiya took one look at me and criticized me for my careless way of dressing — my head was uncovered in the middle of Ramadan. Then, laughing like a kid who had pulled a clever trick, he showed me an explosive device concealed in a thermos bottle. He had been looking for me, he explained, to show me the proof of the operation. He pulled out a cassette and right there in the car he showed the pictures on his camcorder.

The video, which lasted about ten minutes, showed fighters in fields with their faces hidden by kaffiyehs or white scarves, armed with Kalashnikovs, antitank rocket launchers, and portable SAM-14 missile launchers. You saw first an American helicopter pass through the field of vision of the fighters. A little later, one of the fighters fired a missile that rose into the air, leaving behind a stream of white smoke. I shook my head in disbelief. Right there, in front of my hotel in broad daylight, Abu Abdullah was showing me the film of an attack aimed at an Airbus A300 charted by the DHL courier company! The left wing of the plane had caught fire. Miraculously, the pilot had somehow managed to land the plane at the Baghdad airport, with no casualties. After the attack, the Jordanian company Royal Wings, the only one with an airline connected to Baghdad, would decide to suspend flights to the Iraqi capital.

Because he liked me, and because he knew Muhammad, the Salafist fighter had decided to trust me. I also think he wanted to show possible Saudi financiers what he was capable of. The "resistance" was beginning to need money. He therefore turned over the unedited cassette to me. In the film you could clearly see the faces of the fighters, his in particular. As he handed me the cassette, Abu Abdullah asked me to conceal the faces when the film was edited. I wondered if he was aware of the difficult situation he was putting me in. First, I failed totally to understand why he would entrust me with an "unedited" film. Second, the "emir" who had fired the missile at the plane and his entourage could take offense at the power I suddenly held over them. Third, if the coalition heard about it, they would surely want to get their hands on this piece of evidence and interrogate me. In my hotel room, where I had returned to finish an article, I was so nervous and unnerved that I jumped at every gunshot and explosion that rang out in the city.

Even in "normal" times at the Hotel al-Hamra, it was easy to give in to frequent pangs of anxiety. Something was always happening: when we weren't wearily looking out our windows at gray plumes of smoke from explosions, the order spread that all the reporters in the hotel would have to decamp because of rumors of an imminent attack. The night I arrived in Baghdad, as I was heading up to my room, all the war reporters were racing out of the hotel, so I ended up taking refuge with my friend Jabbar's brother. And even there, gunshots exploded right beneath our windows. A few days before the DHL story, the firing of Kalashnikovs had been so intense that we all took refuge in the hotel corridors, as far from the vulnerable windows as possible. The resident private guards, convinced we were under siege, were trembling in their boots. It turned out the firing was in celebration of a victory in a nearby soccer match.

On this particular evening, I felt the enormous responsibility of the videocassette, and wondered what I should do with it. Muhammad and I consulted with Paul, a Lebanese photographer who had been working with us for the last few days. Muhammad had become irrational, subject to frequent panic attacks. He told me that his wife had dreamed that my daughter was mourning my death. He was so anxious, he recommended we deep-six the cassette. Used to his emotional outbursts, I reassured him and decided to ask the advice of the Agence France-Presse bureau chief, Sammy Katz, an experienced reporter who had been covering the Middle East for decades. Paul and I hopped on the old Norton motorcycle, once owned by an apparatchik of the old regime, that he had found in a garage. For some time now, since the rise of religious fundamentalism in Iraq, the appearance of a couple on a motorcycle had been barred, and we were hardly inconspicuous as we drove down the Baghdad streets. To make matters worse, we ran out of gas. Terrified at the danger we posed to his business, the gas station owner let us in ahead of the long line of drivers, who were so taken aback by our appearance that they didn't even bother to protest. I appreciated the outing. Motorcycles had always given me a feeling of freedom, and I was reminded of driving around Paris at night. For the moment, at least, I stopped thinking about the consequences of the decision I had to make.

At the AFP office the discussion was heated. Everyone had advice to give, and no two opinions were the same. Should the cassette be broadcast, sold, given to someone? To whom? Could the coalition have the press agency's bureau closed for disseminating enemy propaganda? Everyone was talking at once; my head was spinning.

The Anglo-Saxons advised me to sell the cassette; they couldn't understand my scruples. The French, always suspicious of money, disapproved. A major American network to whom we had shown the cassette offered me a stack of dollars. They pursued me on the staircase with arguments like: "The war is being paid for by American taxpayers, so an American network should get those pictures." Tempers rose, and so did the bidding for this exclusive footage. I found myself moved into a world ruled by the commercial logic of scoop and of television. I had the uncomfortable impression I was transporting cocaine in my bag, a sack of deadly powder worth a fortune. If I decided to sell the pictures, I could get hundreds of thousands of dollars for a video lasting a few minutes that would be out of date as soon as it was broadcast.

After a night of tossing and turning, I decided that the cassette was a piece of information that ought to be broadcast. The AFP bureau chief advised me to give it to a French public network and to the BBC, to anyone who wanted to broadcast it. In fact CBS, associated with a French network, was the first to broadcast the tape. My editor in Paris, René Backmann, continued to receive fabulous money offers for the cassette. Everyone would soon be able to broadcast the pictures for free, he kept saying, but no one listened. Dollar offers kept coming in. I was besieged in my hotel room in Baghdad by a constant stream of reporters asking me for the notorious cassette or for an interview.

From al-Jazeera to Fox TV, from China to South America, television stations around the world would broadcast the pictures of Abu Abdullah, "warrior" for some, "terrorist" for others. He was the first to have come close to bringing down a civilian aircraft in Iraq. I smiled, remembering Abu Abdullah, the insurgent lost in the countryside of Iraq who complained he couldn't even find arms caches buried in the squash fields of the Sunni Triangle.

ABOVE: March/April 2003. U.S. troops have just taken Tikrit. Marines, smiling after their conquest, ask me to pose for a "victory photo." *(Stephane Faris)*

BELOW LEFT: August 2003. Water shortages in Baghdad are endemic. When an attack blows up a water main, the inhabitants of Baghdad seize the chance to swim and wash their cars. *(Yan Gilbert)*

BELOW RIGHT: August 2003. In the streets of Fallujah. *(Yan Gilbert)*

March 30, 2004. Photographer Stanley Greene and I have arrived in Fallujah after the murder of the four American contractors. Near the burning hulks of the contractors' cars, a man holds a poster that reads "Fallujah, the Americans' cemetery." *(Stanley Greene)*

March 30, 2004. A group of men has just brought down the bodies of two civilian contractors who were hanged and then burned, to further desecrate their charred remains. *(Stanley Greene)*

ABOVE: April 2004. Partisans of Muqtada al-Sadr protest the closure of the movement's newspaper by the Americans. *(Stanley Greene)*

BELOW: April 2004. Dr. Jenan Hassan, head of the Leukemia Department of Pediatrics at the Basra hospital. *(Stanley Greene)*

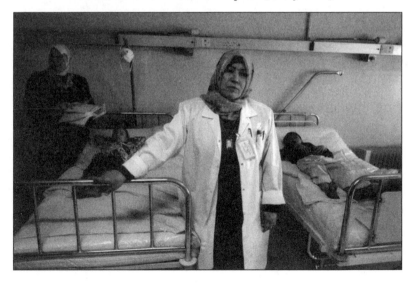

ABOVE: April 2004. An Iraqi woman holding her child, at Najaf gate. She lives in a district where houses are built out of the city's detritus. *(Stanley Greene)*

BELOW: April 2004. Najaf burial in the City of the Dead. *(Stanley Greene)*

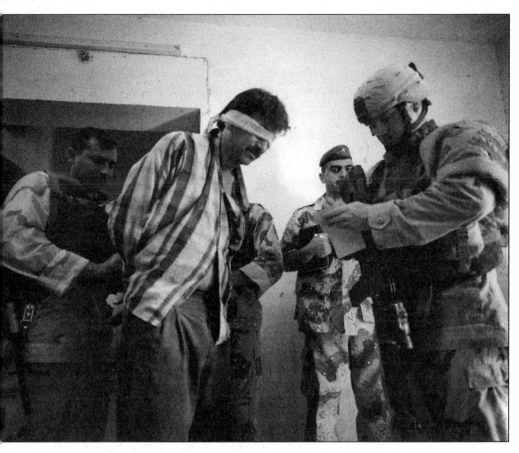

June 2005. After an attack near Baquba, American soldiers hand over Iraqi soldiers, who have been taken prisoner, to be interrogated. *(Stanley Greene)*

June 2005. An Iraqi policeman at a frequently attacked checkpoint in the region of Baquba. *(Stanley Greene)*

June 2005. Mass grave in the desert between Baquba and Baghdad. Soldiers pick up body parts and any other evidence that might identify the victims. *(Stanley Greene)*

June 2005. Evangelical Christian service for American soldiers in FOB warehouse. *(Stanley Greene)*

Reporter saw insurgents loot Qaqaa arms depot

A French journalist who visited the Qaqaa munitions depot south of Baghdad in November last year said she witnessed Islamic insurgents looting vast supplies of explosives more than six months after the demise of Saddam Hussein's regime. . . .

A man who identified himself as Abu Abdullah and led the group [Sara] Daniel was with told her that his men and numerous other insurgent groups had rushed to Qaqaa after U.S.-led troops captured Baghdad. . . . The groups stole truck-loads of material from what used to be the biggest explosive factory in the Middle East in the expectation that coalition forces would move quickly to seal it off, Daniel was told. . . .

But much to the insurgents' surprise, Qaqaa was not sealed off by U.S. soldiers, leading many groups to stop hoarding and instead going for regular refills of explosive materials, according to Abu Abdullah. . . .

Daniel said those who went to Qaqaa to stock up on munitions appeared ready to use them to attack the occupying forces. On Nov. 22, a few days after her visit at Qaqaa, Abu Abdullah's group fired a surface-to-air missile at a DHL cargo-plane. The men gave her a video tape of themselves launching the attack.

—International Herald Tribune

I was in Qaqaa when I witnessed insurgents openly looting the arms depot.
The next day, I broke the news worldwide. (*International Herald Tribune*)

ABOVE: June 2005. Sergeant Ladisic next to his Humvee, damaged by an IED (improvised explosive device) and never completely repaired. *(Stanley Greene)*

BELOW: June 2005. Sergeant Escoffery and Nicole Paquin at Forward Operations Base Speicher in Tikrit. *(Stanley Greene)*

7

With the 101st Airborne
November 2003

FTER MY NERVE-RACKING SOJOURN with the insurgents, I
yearned to report from the other side, and I asked to be
embedded for a few days with the American army. The
Coalition Provisional Authority informed me by e-mail that Paul
and I had been accepted by the 101st Airborne Division in Mosul, very good news. Reporters generally chose places more
familiar to the general public, such as Baghdad or Fallujah. General David Petraeus, head of the 101st, had a reputation among
reporters as an enlightened officer. He had adopted different
methods, and the men of the 101st, along with the British, were
the only ones who dared patrol on foot the streets of an Iraqi city
known as the birthplace of many of Saddam's generals. Under
Petraeus, and perhaps because of him, Mosul was relatively
quiet, and I was glad to return to a region I had visited earlier in
the war.*

When we got to Mosul, after driving five hours on a dusty
and uneventful road, I recognized the "hotel" where I had tried
to get a room during the war. Then, while I had been waiting at
the reception desk, gangs of looters were sacking the building.
They had done good work: the hotel resembled an empty warehouse, a huge space open to the elements. I found it hard to believe that the American army had camped its soldiers in this frigid,
devastated place. The soldiers had set up their cots wherever

---

* It was later to become a guerrilla stronghold.

they could, sheltered by blankets stretched out along the windows to protect them from the cold wind coming through the broken windows. How was it that the 101st, one of the most prestigious divisions of the American army, didn't have better living conditions? Paul and I settled into a small room on the top floor of the hotel. Our sleeping bags were set on a thick layer of filth, and there was no glass in the windows, but we felt lucky, for we had the supreme luxury of being alone. The one neighbor on our floor, an excitable and slightly paranoid sergeant of about forty, told us every night that the battle to drive back an offensive against headquarters would come that night.

The Apache helicopters of the 101st had fired the first shots in Operation Desert Storm in 1991. In this war, they had fought battles in Najaf and Nasiriya before getting to Baghdad. After taking up quarters in this city in northern Iraq, they were as surprised as everyone else by the speed of victory. They had suffered no deaths during the war; it was only later that things turned bad. Now, day after day, soldiers of the 101st fell under the bullets of insurgents. Their support weapons and training provided no protection against explosive devices laid by faceless enemies.

In my few days with the Iraqi insurgents, I had learned a lot. As I patrolled with the soldiers, because of my recent education in the insurgent camp, I would be far more acutely aware than they of the dangers threatening us. By its contradictory experiences, the job was making me schizophrenic. Juxtaposing all the different pictures confirmed to me that in this war everything depended on your point of view. Each day in Iraq brought home to me the fact that the war was becoming harsher and dirtier, that there was no right side, no heroes, only victims.

The very next day, still with the 101st Airborne Division, I attended a service commemorating the dead, conducted with an imposing sense of ceremony. It was sad and moving, tragically real.

When it came to the religious part of the ceremony, I felt ill at ease. It all seemed surreal to me when the grief-stricken soldiers mentioned God's purpose guiding their hands against the enemy. Only days earlier, Iraqi insurgents had tried to convert

me to their cause and their God. The words used by these enemies were oddly similar, apparently from another era, the age of
Savonarola and Saladin. If the religiosity of the moment made
me feel ill at ease, I was particularly moved by the tears flowing
down the craggy face of General Petraeus. This man who led
one of the most prestigious divisions of the most powerful army
in the world seemed at that moment lost inside a uniform too
large for him. All the officers had respectfully stepped away from
him, surprised by his open show of mourning. For a long time,
the general stared at the procession of his men who had come to
pay their last respects to the soldiers killed in the collision of two
helicopters over Mosul hit by a rocket-propelled grenade. With
seventeen dead and five wounded, this was the deadliest attack so
far against American soldiers since the official end of hostilities
in Iraq on May 1.

That evening, when I spoke with General Petraeus in his
headquarters in Saddam's former palace in Mosul, I realized that
I had attributed my own questions to him. Did the tears I found
so surprising in a soldier accustomed to the risks of his job come
from his doubts? Did he wonder what purpose was served by the
death of men forcing their way into a country that did not want
them? The general, to my surprise and despite his emotion, did
not have a shred of doubt about the justification for the war. "I
think this generation of Americans is really amazing. They're
marvelous, you know," he told me. You could just read between
the lines that he would have liked to have more resources to re-
construct "his" region.

Later in the ceremony, a soldier called the roll of the living
and the dead: "Sergeant Acklin, Sergeant Michael Acklin, Sergeant Michael D. Acklin." The name of each dead soldier was
read out amid the names of the living. And in the silence greet-
ing the call, many of the parachutists of the 101st wept as their
commander had.

I observed the soldiers who came forward to speak in memory of their comrades. Like all the men present at the ceremony,
they had been there from the very first days of the war. They had

spent seven long months in intimate contact with death and boredom. "Some people wonder why we're still in Iraq," one of them said. "They forget that since September 11 there have been no terrorist attacks in the United States. These men who have died had faith in the most powerful nation on earth. God, this hurts! But you are heroes who have fallen to save the world. I love you, my friends, and I'll see you in heaven." The soldiers needed to believe that their comrades had died to avenge September 11 and to make sure it didn't happen again. Every speech called on God. "We'll meet in heaven. . . . We'll get to the promised land." God was everywhere. They were fighting in His name, and He justified the ultimate sacrifice. When the time came, He would explain everything that seemed incoherent. This was simple and convenient, and made it possible to have patience. This sounded ironically similar to the impassioned words of Muslim suicide bombers. All one had to do was substitute God for Allah.

A sergeant from Mexico, John Paul Garcia, placed a little cross next to the boots of his friend Michael Acklin, dead at twenty-five. He thanked me emotionally for listening to him. He looked young and vulnerable. He didn't really know why he was there or why his friend had died. "These people don't want to be free. Everybody hates us. I don't understand." Every day, Garcia told me, he prayed for himself and for the enemies of America. He kept a rosary, which never left his side, in the case with his earplugs. He pulled a photograph of his late mother out of the left breast pocket of his uniform. "She is my guardian angel, she and the good Lord." I asked him why he thought the American army was in Iraq. "Acklin, my friend who just died, thought that God had given us a mission. The rest of it is nothing but dirty politics." The sergeant was tired of mourning his comrades. A few days earlier one of his men had had a leg blown off by an explosive device while at the wheel of a Humvee. "I was supposed to be driving, but I was assigned somewhere else. When I saw that twenty-one-year-old kid amputated up to the thigh, I said to

him: 'Oh Leo, if only I could have been in your place!' And you
know what he answered? 'No, John, you have a wife and kids, it's
better that it happened to me.'"

One morning Paul and I got up at five. A platoon of ten soldiers
was setting out on foot patrol on the large main road of Mosul.
For five minutes we debated whether we would go with them.
Foot patrols, we knew, were about the most dangerous places to
be. Was it worth it for three lines in an article? I of course knew
the answer: To describe with depth and accuracy what these men
were experiencing and feeling, you had to do what they did. So we
followed them. We advanced in the open across the median between the two strips of the main road in Mosul. Walking between
two soldiers, my nerves raw, I jumped at every dog that barked in
the dawn silence. That morning I wasn't wearing my bulletproof
vest and felt terribly vulnerable on this deserted road, at the
mercy of a grenade or a bullet. I couldn't believe that just a few
short days before I had been working alongside anti-American insurgents. What a strange profession, my war reporting! I knew
their weapons, the ease with which they could hit their targets,
and their predilection for early morning. During the entire patrol
I tried, like the soldiers, not to think of what might happen to us.
They kept marching ahead. How far was it reasonable to go?
Again, was it worth risking my life for two or three lines, at most
a paragraph? Too late to think about that now. Walking down that
road, I could think of nothing but being cold, hungry, and tired.
The soldiers with us stopped cars, inspected suspicious materials
and threatening shapes. Every pile of gravel was turned over. A
pack of stray dogs following the patrol was the only distraction we
encountered. It was extremely tedious and, as I began sharing the
soldiers' feelings, boredom and sheer fatigue soon overwhelmed
my fear. Frozen stiff, we counted the steps separating us from
headquarters in the Hotel Mosul. On the front door I noticed a
sign I hadn't seen on the way out, saying: "The people of our
country can sleep peacefully in their beds at night only because

warriors are willing to use violence for them. Let them sleep."
Soldiers still thought they were fighting to protect the domestic
security of the United States.

Back in the camp, I stopped to exchange a few words with
our neighbor Sergeant Harris, petting a black-and-white puppy,
grasping a few moments of tenderness. He was at the end of his
rope, tired of the whole mess. He had unstitched his name tag
from his jacket so the enemy couldn't find it, convinced the rag-
tag army of Iraqis against whom he was fighting had enough
connections to be able to find his family in the United States.
Like so many, he kept repeating that the September 11 terrorists
and the Iraqi insurgents belonged to a single network. He
loathed Iraq, which he did not understand. "These people don't
give a shit about rebuilding their country. The place is full of
bastards who think only of themselves. They don't even have
gardens." His only consolation in Iraq was his close friend from
Chicago, thirty-one-year-old Sergeant Mario Bievre. "We just
want to survive day by day. I take care of him and he takes care of
me. I know everything about him, his faults, his habits." For
Bievre, his fellow sufferer, the hardest thing was the monotony.
"Day after day, it's the same thing. They shoot at us in the middle
of the night. We take up position. We're not even afraid anymore, we just want to stay in bed."

Our stomachs were growling when the breakfast wagon finally arrived at 7:30. The one memory that sticks out from the
time I spent with the men of the 101st was the constant cold and
hunger. The men complained a lot about the food. Barely standing, soldiers gulped down grayish scrambled eggs and stale bread.

Captain Steve Cunningham, twenty eight years old, in charge
of 130 men, was scrupulous about the rules: no leave during the
fighting, not a drop of beer, and no pornographic pictures — all
the girls decorating the walls of the rooms were in bathing suits.
Any violator incurred severe penalties, extra duties dragging out
an exhausting day. For serious offenses, the penalty was forty-
five days of extra service. "But that's unusual, because soldiers
don't have time to break rules," Cunningham assured me. There

was no downtime in the 101st. On the wall was a small poster warning soldiers against the effects of Valium, which some soldiers asked the translators to supply them with. For this ambitious West Point graduate, the rules were just as restrictive. He had not seen his wife for eight months, even though she too was in the 101st in Mosul, in a unit on the other side of town. "Two ships passing in the night," he sighed. Whenever he had a free minute, he would send her an e-mail. After a while, connections between couples frayed. I watched as soldiers ended up fighting with their wives, left alone to take care of things for months at a time.

"It can't be, we're not crazy enough to do this!" shouted the soldiers as we started out on patrol one day. I was thinking the same thing, sitting in a truck, with no guarantee that I'd get anything to write out of it. "Yes, we are. We're tough and we're heading out!" they shouted. And it seemed to work — you felt braver with everyone yelling at once.

In the truck there were eight, nine with me, encased in bulletproof vests, their pockets full of soldier's equipment, their hands on their M-16s. I was inwardly very scared, because I knew that patrolling by truck was highly dangerous. I did not fully appreciate the ride. The men who knew full well what they were risking, who had seen several comrades get blown to bits, soon grew quiet. Amputation, even more than death itself, was the great fear of soldiers in Iraq. Seated on a bench fastened in the middle of the vehicle, we were perfect targets, at the mercy of grenades and explosive devices. Since attacks had resumed, soldiers had nailed boards on the sides of the vehicle to absorb shell fragments. I smiled at this kind of do-it-yourself protection, hardly suggesting that we were in the "greatest army in the world."

Piled one on top of another, we could hardly keep upright every time we went over a bump. Sergeant Joseph Kramer yelled at the man next to him, whose mess kit had jabbed the sergeant's eye. As for me, the long strip of bullets for the truck's machine gun landed heavily on my shoulder, but I didn't dare budge, much less complain. "Of course, I'm afraid of bombs. Soon, you know, we're going to leave. We're not going to spend our lives as living targets." Occupation wasn't for Joseph Kramer; he missed the "good time" of war. They were the three hardest weeks of his life. "We had to march for whole days with huge packs on our backs and then fight, but at least we knew why we were there," he explained. "But the violence really happened here in Mosul. Since 'they' got reorganized." Joseph described the frustration of an elite force confronting guerrilla fighters. "Attacks can come from hundreds of places and we can't do anything about it. Our life in Iraq is like *Groundhog Day*. We get up, we get shot at, we go to bed, and it starts over again, over and over, never stopping." This handsome soldier with his clear blue eyes harshly criticized orders from the high command. The litany continued. "Frankly, I don't see where we're going. This insurgency is like gang warfare in the States. To fight it, we'd have to be a sophisticated police force, which we're not." He had nothing but contempt for the Iraqi police. "When we take them out on patrol, we have to tell them everything. And besides, they're so ignorant! The other day, for instance, one of them didn't even know that Israel was a country! I had to show him on a map. And we're supposed to be handing over to them the keys to Iraq someday soon!"

This day the patrol had to go with a fine-toothed comb through the neighborhood where a Black Hawk helicopter had been shot down. It was a poor area, most of whose inhabitants had worked at the Pepsi-Cola factory owned by Saddam's despised son Uday. Since Operation Steel Hammer, sporadic house searches had resumed. A small column of soldiers moved forward. One of the men knocked violently on an iron door, which buckled under his fist. I was behind six American soldiers and the same number of Iraqi policemen, who plunged into the corridor pointing their weapons. The scene was extremely violent, and I found it hard to separate myself from the intruders. All the inhabitants of the house looked at me with hatred, convinced I was working with the soldiers, either as an interpreter or to search the women. The soldiers swarmed over the patio of the little house, searched the rooms, climbed the stairs. A three-year-old girl, suddenly awakened by the intrusion of an armed soldier, started to sob. My photographer, Paul, took shots of weapons inches away from babies, which were to become symbolic pictures of the American occupation of Iraq.

Surprised in her private space, one of the women of the house had thrown a bath towel over her head. She held on to my hand because I was a woman, asking me for advice. This wasn't my role, I knew, but how could I resist the desire to comfort her? I patted her gently on the arm and told her that everything would be all right. "I have only one weapon to defend myself," she protested, brandishing the cartridge clips from her Kalashnikov. "OK, but don't let your kids play with it," said the soldier beside me, trying to be friendly.

At the end of the street, the patrol took aim at the poor kids playing on a rusted carousel. "The terrorists sometimes give them a few dinars to throw grenades at us," explained Captain Cunningham. While soldiers ran shouting into the houses, the captain was talking with the neighborhood mayor and questioning the inhabitants. He wrote down their complaints in a little notebook, asked about the father of a resident who was in prison, and about the price of propane. The captain asked after the health of a local sheikh, shook hands with children who cheered him, and politely listened to "information" about terrorists from a woman who appeared disturbed, and who ended the conversation by giving him a noisy kiss on the cheek. He even sat down with her to listen to her chatter and ate the candy she offered him. It was hardly effective, but it was nice. Thanks to these methods, Mosul regained a few weeks of calm. The soldiers of General Petraeus had managed to win hearts and minds, a phrase that would soon become grotesque. But the men of the 101st had shown that the American army could handle itself differently in Iraq and perhaps succeed.

Suddenly a Humvee joined the column of American army vehicles blocking the neighborhood. Colonel Joseph Anderson, commander of the Second Brigade, had come to check on his men's work. With his shaven head and steely blue eyes, he was straight out of Hollywood central casting. In fact, he had become a television star, since he was the one who had coordinated the raid on Saddam's sons' house. The colonel shook a few hands and exchanged pleasantries with the Iraqi police. He too was proud of the methods of the 101st in Mosul. "We're pragmatic. Here, money is our main friend. Of course, sometimes the coalition authority yanks the leash a little. Nobody will ever know this place like the 101st." He was right, and the violence that is now ravaging Mosul makes me wonder if I haven't prettified my memories of those few weeks.

After more than five hours searching houses in the neighborhood, the patrol returned to Second Brigade headquarters. The soldiers went to their quarters or played a video football game, "the only thing that keeps us from going crazy here," joked Sergeant Kramer. When he wasn't watching the brigade's favorite movie, *Black Hawk Down,* on his portable DVD player, Joseph Kramer liked to read. On top of the mess kit next to his cot was his favorite book, *Why Do People Hate America?* published by Disinformation Books. Two weeks earlier he had stopped reading the *New York Times* and started consulting the Web pages of the *Washington Post.* "I had had enough of reading only negative things about the army. No one talks about the good things we do. Like the time a schoolteacher started to cry when we gave her fifty dollars." Sergeant Kramer described himself as a liberal, the kind of soldier with more questions than answers. He knew Americans had faults, but they were a thousand times better than Saddam. "Sometimes I tell myself we should leave like some people here demand, and we'd soon see Iraqis begging us to come back. But I think now that we've come into the country, we have a responsibility even to those who don't share our ideas." Kramer, who claimed not to be a great fan of unilateralism, had had many doubts about the necessity of the war. "I don't understand how Iraq got to be part of the axis of evil." It was Powell's speech that had convinced him of the necessity for a preventive war. "As a soldier, I was used to the idea of obeying orders that I didn't necessarily agree with. And also, as a Democrat, I think it's important to serve your country. That lets us send people packing when they claim we're not patriotic. When I get back to the United States, I'll be able to explain to those good folks how complicated this part of the world is." As for his mission in Iraq, he had only one wish: that it be over. "Let me be clear: This job is hard, it's creepy. We're sacrificing ourselves for a mission we don't understand. Our only hope is to believe that our leaders know what they're doing."

Night finally fell on the camp. Soldiers not on watch could catch a few hours' sleep. I got back to my room next to the one belonging to Corporal Harris. The solitary soldier again came to warn me. That night, he was sure, was the one; the camp was going to be attacked by the enemy. He was preparing his weapons, and asked where we wanted to be when the attack came. In fact, that night only a few Kalashnikov rounds and a distant mortar shell disturbed the silence. But, as he did every night, the soldier was dreaming of open warfare face to face with the enemy, far from video games, e-mails, and faceless foes, far from this Iraqi quagmire where only death did not seem virtual.

8

Captain Elliott
November 2003

I MET ROGER ELLIOTT, a captain in the reserve, one day in November 2003 in the town hall in Sadr City. He was taking the first steps toward setting up a local council for the sprawling Shiite slum in eastern Baghdad, formerly known as Saddam City, now renamed in honor of the extremist leader Muqtada al-Sadr by his followers. Roger was one of the few American army officers who had not made me feel that I was suspect because I was French. He didn't sneer or display the distrust that so often greeted my compatriots, at least at first, whenever they approached American installations.

During the March offensive in Mosul, a few hours after the city was liberated from Saddam's regime, an American major named David Grosso had made it clear to me that coalition forces would never forget the insult inflicted on them by their former allies. "Tell your French readers that we Americans will never forget: not Normandy and not this betrayal," he thundered, staring at me fiercely. This was the only statement I got from the major; he preferred answering questions from my American colleague from *Newsday*, with whom I had traveled from Baghdad. It was no good claiming that reporters were impartial — I soon learned that, for American soldiers as for Iraqi insurgents, the nationality on your passport classified you immediately as ally or enemy.

Captain Elliott had graciously responded to my questions from the very beginning. In fact, he himself was full of questions about the other Iraq, the country that American soldiers never saw, about "my" war and the time I had spent with his enemies. For an entire day, my photographer Paul, my driver Muhammad, and I observed him negotiating the price of cooking gas with a tribal leader dressed in black. The price of this gas, which was vital for the population, had skyrocketed since the war. The sheikh was one of the organizers of the black market and had no desire to see his profit reduced. Elliott talked for hours about the common good of the Iraqis and explained to the doubtful tribal leader why what he was doing was illegal in the new Iraq. He sang the praises of the coupon system. His interpreter Imad, a beautiful thirty-seven-year-old Palestinian American, whispered her translations into the ear of the impassive Iraqi. Worn out after several hours, she got up to take a break. Turning to me and smiling indulgently at the captain, she said, "He doesn't understand that he's wasting his time. Things don't work like that with us Arabs."

We insisted on talking with the beautiful Imad, a gym teacher in the Midwest who had left her husband and children to serve in Iraq. My driver Muhammad especially wanted to understand. This was the first time he had been in an American installation and spoken to soldiers who smiled back at him, in contrast to the brutality at checkpoints and the frequent searches of his house. But that day the enemy had the enchanting face of a woman belonging to a fraternal people who had also suffered. At first she flatly refused. Shaking her thick brown curls, she said that all reporters were manipulators and she was tired of being insulted by Iraqis in the street because she wore the insignia of the invader. She then softened and wanted to justify herself, and so a dialogue was engaged between the Palestinian and the Iraqi.

"How can you wear the uniform of the American army that invaded your brothers' land?"

"We came to help you. I decided to join up and leave my children because I felt helpless and could do nothing for my own uprooted and victimized people. Being here, I have the sense that I'm helping my brothers."

"What help are you talking about? My wife and children can't even leave the house anymore because they're too afraid. And the neighborhood mosque supplies the little bit of electricity we get."

"Are you telling me that the situation is worse today than under Saddam?"

"Yes, I swear to God it is."

The Palestinian's eyes brimmed with tears, and Muhammad changed the subject. "Can you help me get a weapons permit?"

"I'll fix it with the captain."

I had to beg Captain Elliott not to grant his request, to avoid the risk of seeing my companion empty his weapon into a driver who might irritate him.

Around six we shared dinner with the soldiers in the mess hall of Camp Marlboro. It was Iftar, the hour when the fast is broken during the month of Ramadan, and despite his hesitation I had persuaded Muhammad, who had eaten and drunk nothing since five in the morning, to come with us. In the mess hall, plunged into total darkness because of a power failure, it felt as though we were at a wake. The most surprising thing was the complete silence in which the soldiers ate. We stood on line to get a scoop of nauseating mashed potatoes, a piece of shoe leather masquerading as a steak, and a flat soda on our plastic trays. Despite his hunger, Muhammad was unable to swallow the revolting food. "You have to write about the lousy food they give the Americans," he ordered me, stunned and saddened, pointing to his plastic knife that had just broken for the second time as he tried to cut his meat.

By the glow of the Maglite set on the table, I ate dinner that evening sitting opposite men who were perhaps the only two Democrats in Camp Marlboro. Captain Allen Vaught, a Dallas lawyer in civilian life, was recuperating at Camp Marlboro from his previous posting in Fallujah, the insurgents' capital, where he had undergone daily attacks. He was waiting for things to be over. He didn't want to die in a war he didn't believe in. He had helped set up a new soccer field for the inhabitants of Fallujah.

The next day, everything was gone — the metal frames of the goals, even the mud on the field. "How can you help people who are willing to steal mud?" he wondered.

Captain Elliott was gloomy, and I recited French poetry to distract him. In this somber and surrealistic gloom, Gérard de Nerval came to me: *"Je suis le ténébreux, le veuf, l'inconsolé . . ."* Fortunately, the captain did not understand French.

I immediately felt close to Roger Elliott. At first sight, he might appear to be as foreign to me, a French atheist, as an Iraqi Islamist would be. He was from Texas and a preacher in the very conservative Church of Christ. Filled with doubts and scruples, he was a renegade who questioned the values and commandments that his background would naturally have brought him to adopt without any qualms. In civilian life he had participated in politics, running tirelessly as a Democrat in an essentially conservative state in races he usually lost. But he had managed to get elected mayor of the town of Hudson Oaks. He had problems with the most conservative members of his congregation, who denied the right of women to serve the church and wanted to exclude homosexuals and divorced persons.

I asked him over and over why he hadn't decided to leave a state that was so dull, a church that was so reactionary, and an army that had brought him to wage a war in which he did not believe. He answered the same way every time: you had to try to change things from inside, you had to fight. Skeptical about the conduct of the war and about the reasons given by the Bush administration for starting it, Captain Elliott nevertheless thought he could make a difference in Iraq by his individual behavior. He hadn't wanted to be a conscientious objector, but he reserved the right to make a judgment of conscience about the legitimacy of any order he might be given. His men had described the captain as a hero to me. One of them told me the story of an attack during which Elliott had thrown himself on top of an Iraqi prisoner to protect him from bullets with his own body. "I can tell you that wouldn't have been *my* first reaction," admitted Sergeant Billy Moore, who had witnessed the attack. Elliott thought a man of honor had to try to make up for the aberrations of the army by his conduct. The captain judged his fellow soldiers harshly — like the group that had abused some Iraqi women whom they had invited to "party" in spite of the protests of the men with them, or like a certain other captain who boasted that he wouldn't call his parents unless he could tell them that he had humiliated an Iraqi. Elliott had been assigned to replace this captain, who had killed an impressive number of the enemy. He had been dismissed from the army for provoking a riot in Sadr City by ordering his men to take down one of the black flags that are the sacred banner of the Shiites. The riot had caused several deaths, including that of a child.

When I met Elliott, the atmosphere in the Sadr City town hall was extremely tense. A few days before our visit, sentries guarding the entrance had shot the head of the local council, Muhammad, who had refused to be searched, demanding to be treated like the Americans who had appointed him to the position. He wanted to be shown the respect owed to his office. The business had shocked Iraqis all the more because he had been picked by the Americans to replace another official who was more of an extremist and more hostile to them.

The captain did not evade my questions. He even confessed to some admiration for his Iraqi colleague in Sadr City: "Muhammad stood up to us, which is a good thing, a little like the French who said no to us in the Security Council. We didn't liberate the Iraqis so they could become our lackeys."

Muhammad's right-hand man, who had witnessed the leader's killing, refused to talk to me in front of the soldiers in the council chamber. He took me into a small room to give me his version of events. On November 8 at eleven in the morning, Muhammad had come back to the town hall after inspecting trash collection in Sadr City. A soldier had asked him to get out of his car, turn over his weapon, and submit to a search. Muhammad had called over an officer and told him: "I'm the head of the municipal council, and this is my building. If you don't let me go in, I'll never set foot here again." The officer had prohibited him from getting back into his car. With the new mobile phone the Americans had given him, Muhammad called an American adviser to the council. The officer in charge was not there, but Muhammad had been able to talk to the Palestinian interpreter and to a superior who told him he could enter the building. When he returned, the soldier told him to turn back. "But I have permission from your superior," Muhammad said, annoyed. The soldier pushed him back. Muhammad grabbed the soldier by the hand and twisted it. Behind him, a soldier fired in the air. The second bullet hit him in the hip. At that point, the interpreter came out to intervene, but it was too late. The head of the council died on the way to the hospital.

This was one of those tragic and stupid accidents that happened daily and increased the hatred and suspicion between the Americans and Iraqis. Elliott liked to believe that, had he been present, things would have gone differently.

When I saw Elliott again in June 2004 in Houston, where I had come to interview soldiers who had returned home, the captain was still haunted by the same questions. Because he was troubled by insomnia and woke up perspiring, army doctors thought he was suffering from post-traumatic stress disorder caused by the danger he had faced. For his part, Elliott believed that his stress came from the contradictions he had to manage daily while doing his "duty" in Iraq, and especially the unknown faces of Iraqis he had killed. He was obsessed by these images. Over and over, he tortured himself, relentlessly picturing what they might have become, what their favorite food was, the pain of their relatives. How could you kill in the name of a mission you doubted when you believed in God? This was among the few questions the captain couldn't answer.

One image that continued to obsess him was of the man who could not bring himself to bury his child. Seeing this Iraqi carrying around the corpse of his child day after day had broken his heart. Then there were the pictures of Elliot's wounded and mutilated comrades, like that soldier named Kelly who had lost one of his legs. When I reached Kelly by telephone, he was on the point of crying because he had gotten a flat on the way to Walter Reed Hospital and had to wait for someone to come and help him — a twenty-five-year-old kid who couldn't even change a tire!

And yet Captain Elliott missed Iraq, the adrenaline fix it had given him, the feeling he was accomplishing great things, driving his Humvee, danger. A reporter had photographed Elliott when he was wounded in an attack. Back in Texas, he'd had a painting made from the photograph. You could see him in the painting spotted with blood, looking completely different. Enormous power emanated from this picture of a man who had tested his limits, who had exposed himself to the danger of being killed by a bomb, but also to the danger of losing face, of running away, who had once again conquered his fear.

What was life like for a homecoming hero, a veteran of Iraq?

One month after his return, Elliott had found a job in Houston, about a five-hour drive from his home in Fort Worth. Burdened by mortgage and car payments, he had to reduce all his expenses. So, to economize, he had moved back in with his parents. At night after work, he kept his grandfather company. At thirty-five, the hero was back in his childhood home.

When his work in a lawyer's office and his military training left him the time, he went to see his wife and children, about one weekend out of two. There he spent all of Sunday at church, where he was a deacon, listening to other people's problems.

What is it that makes a man different? How is it that in a Manichaean world where good guys face bad guys, some men keep asking questions, feeling doubts? Hour after hour, I questioned the captain, intrigued by this Sisyphean warrior who thought that despite the futility of his task he had to carry it out day after day without stopping, and who had assured me that if he were sent back to Iraq, he would do his "duty."

Elliott had been adopted at the age of five. His father, who had three wives and three mistresses, had been the guru of a hippie commune of the kind that flourished in the 1960s and '70s, and had abused his own children. His mother had not wanted to leave the sect and finally resigned herself to having him adopted. She had set two conditions, which she pinned to his blanket when she deposited Roger and his sister at an orphanage. The children could not be separated, and they were to be raised according to the precepts of the very conservative Church of Christ.

What surprised me in the captain was his ability to accept the constraints imposed on him and his determination to change things from the inside. He had now moved away from the precepts of his church. He no longer went there three times a week, and he was no longer a deacon in Fort Worth. He asserted, however, that his faith had never been stronger and that he still prayed out loud. But he had moved some distance from the religiosity and the dogma of the church.

I saw Roger Elliott again several times. Over the many months we had known each other during the Iraq war, we had become close friends. I made a trip to Houston to see him, and at one point he in turn came to Paris to pay me a visit. He even went so far as to travel to London at my request, for I wanted him to meet another man I admired, who was nonetheless at the other end of the political spectrum, Dr. Salam, a Salafist who had taken a leave of absence from the war to recuperate in Britain.

In my naïveté, I had felt that my two friends, whom circumstances had turned into enemies, might profit from a meeting on common ground. But the encounter between the Texan minister of the Church of Christ and the Iraqi jihadist physician was a total failure. I kept copious notes during their meeting, which went on for several days. In rereading this dialogue of the deaf, I realized what an immense, virtually insurmountable gulf separated them.

Roger spoke with the pragmatic self-assurance of a man who belonged to a society that fashioned, if not dominated, the world. By contrast, Salam's world was filled with bitterness and fear, the history of his people one long and unjust sequence of domination and dictatorship. I knew we were in trouble when, in Roger's presence, Salam could not conceal that the attack on the

Twin Towers had been for him a moment of pure pleasure and satisfaction.

During these long discussions, there was not a moment when I detected a spark of recognition or understanding of the other's viewpoint, not one moment of grace. Earlier, Dr. Salam had privately voiced to me his doubts about some of the tactics the Islamist guerrillas were using, but to Roger he refused even to contemplate the possible error of their ways. And Roger had likewise refused in Salam's presence to voice serious doubts about the American conduct of the war or to address any of its terrible consequences.

The only respite — and it was slight — was when Roger suffered a nasty fall, and to stop the bleeding Dr. Salam gave him a coagulant shot. Even then, before he administered it, he could not help saying, half jokingly, "I'll only give you this shot if you agree on the spot to leave my country immediately."

I had arranged this meeting with high hopes that some mutual understanding, some insights, might emerge from it, for both men were intelligent, sensitive, and dedicated. But I left them with a feeling not only of disappointment but of deep despair.

9

Allen, Ed, and Ivan: Soldiers Speak
June 2004

I WAS IN A STEAK HOUSE IN FORT WORTH with Roger Elliott and two other captains who had also just come back from Iraq, Allen and Ed. We were talking about our children. I told them that my daughter loved to play war, to the great dismay of my friends, who attributed that to my bad influence. Just as we used to play cowboys and Indians, in her games the bad guys were in turn Bin Laden, Saddam Hussein, or "the Americans." Allen was dismayed that a Western kid could think of Americans as enemies. What had happened to bring us to that point? But my daughter was only four, and to make him feel better, I told him that when she encountered French soldiers in railway stations or airports she would point at them and shout: "Taliban!" The story did not mollify him.

It was seven months since I had met Allen Vaught with Roger on a November evening in Camp Marlboro, one of the American bases in Sadr City in Baghdad. This warm, forthcoming reserve officer was a thirty-two-year-old lawyer from Dallas who appeared genuinely relieved to be ending his service in Sadr City after the stresses he had gone through in Fallujah. I remembered him telling me that he didn't want to die in a war he didn't believe in. He would have things to tell me later, after he left the army, he had said. After going through Fallujah, he joked, he didn't want to face a court-martial.

At the beginning of the war, Allen had been convinced he would be welcomed as a liberator. The hostility of the population

of Fallujah, where he had served before coming to Baghdad, had
left him speechless. "All 250,000 of them hated us. We were attacked at least once every three days." But even though this Democrat hadn't believed in the reasons put forth for going to war,
he had tried to do his best, to help people individually. And then
things turned nasty in Sadr City. This Shiite sector of Baghdad
was no longer an area relatively free of attacks. As he was driving
two young women infected with hepatitis C to a military clinic,
his Humvee was hit by an explosive device and he was seriously
wounded. The army doctors on the scene had not immediately
recognized the gravity of his condition. After returning to the
States with his unit, he was transferred by bus from Fort Bragg
in North Carolina to Texas. "It would be like going by car from
Paris to Moscow." He told me that every bump was torture for
his fractured spinal column.

I met him in New York, where he'd come on a business trip,
and later in his native Texas. Restless, down, haunted by violent
nightmares, he seemed out of place in the New York hotel bar
where I met him. I didn't recognize the happy, carefree soldier I
had known in Sadr City. In fact, many of the soldiers I met after
returning home had become rather cynical, a tendency I always
associated with the French. I was surprised to find it so prevalent
among my American friends.

Allen's spinal column had been fractured in four places, and
it caused him enormous pain. One of his associates told me: "He
takes a lot on himself, it's even hard for him to carry a suitcase,
but he can't manage to get himself demobilized."

Allen did not want to go back to Iraq. "Since the end of the
war, it's become a factory for making terrorists, another Pakistan.
And we've shown our worst face there." As a lawyer, he'd been
shaken by the revelation of torture in Abu Ghraib. He would
never have tolerated the slightest inappropriate gesture toward a
prisoner. When he found out that one of his translators, Zia, was
in league with the insurgents, he was devastated. "I had shown
him pictures of my family and my ranch. I thought he was my

friend, but he wanted to kill me. And yet, until he went to Abu Ghraib, I had shared my food and water with him. At the time, supplies were delayed, and we had only a few swallows of water a day." Allen had visions of being greeted as a savior in Iraq, but his good intentions were thrown back in his face, and he had become soured. This was why I found it so hard to recognize him.

He was very discouraged and had begun proceedings to allow one of his unit's translators to come to Texas. "Two of our other translators have just been assassinated, so I'm going to do my duty by this man, because the situation will not get any better."

In his house in Texas, Allen showed me a photograph of his uncle and his medals: he was a U.S. Air Force officer of German origin who had fought in the Second World War and been taken prisoner by the Nazis. "That's my idea of the American army. I understand his disillusionment. He lives with the glorious memory of a war that has never been considered anything but just, because the Nazi enemy was clearly identified and especially because the opposing forces were roughly equal in strength. There wasn't that extreme disparity in resources the insurgents invoke when they're criticized for the primitive barbarism of their methods." I nodded, thinking of the reactions of American soldiers when they entered Nazi concentration camps: "Now I really know what I was fighting for." There was nothing like that in Iraq, nothing that could reassure soldiers about the rightness of their battle, not even the marines who found the headquarters of the throat slitters in Fallujah, because it was the war itself that produced those methods. I had heard so many soldiers confess their feelings of guilt for the people they had killed in Iraq. You have fewer regrets about taking a life during a war if you are convinced the war is just.

Since he'd been back in Texas, Allen had been driving a big 4x4. On Sundays he'd go hunting with friends on his parents' ranch, shooting at targets or water snakes. He'd kept his M-16 from Iraq and modified it into a semiautomatic. In many ways he was a typical God-fearing, gun-loving Texan. But after Iraq, something was different. When he came back, his mother had hoped that he'd become a strong believer. "I believe in God, but here, if you're a Democrat, people think you hate Jesus Christ. In some churches, pro-choice people aren't allowed to take communion," he said with some bitterness.

In his view, the greatest mistake Americans made in Iraq was "imposing Jeffersonian democracy from one day to the next after a dictatorship. What a joke. I'm just a little cog in the wheel and I knew it wouldn't work."

Across the table in Fort Worth was Ed Palacios, sitting next to his girlfriend. This forty-one-year-old captain, proud to be a Republican, had great presence. He told me that, generation after generation, the men in his family had been soldiers. Ed's greatest disappointment was having failed the test to become a marine because of a foot wound. A soldier to the tips of his fingers, this computer programmer spoke calmly until I asked him about his best memory of the war in Iraq. He burst into tears in front of his fiancée. This was the first time he had brought up this memory since his return. I had at first thought of him as stiff and reticent, thought it would be hard to get him to talk. But I was wrong; he was just trying to contain his sorrow. His tears were contagious, and his sadness and feeling of waste revived many memories of my own friends dead or wounded, in exile or kidnapped, of my own weakness and cowardice.

"Her name was Tiba Ayad," he started. "I was at the town hall in Heet, near the Syrian border, and all the Iraqis looked on me with suspicion. But one man dared to approach me. When I asked him what I could do for him, he asked me to help him take care of his sick child. I was touched that he was so concerned for his daughter's health that he would stand up to the contempt and hostility of the others. Tiba was four, and I liked her immediately. She was suffering from a form of cancer, and the chemotherapy that she had been able to get in Iraq wasn't working. I worked it out so that she could go to Jordan, where the queen is involved in caring for sick children. The helicopter was ready.

The family was overjoyed. But at the last minute we found out that the queen of Jordan wasn't accepting any more children. I then contacted Médecins du Monde, and they asked me to bring her to Baghdad. I went with her in a taxi to the capital. The doctor accepted her, and a plane was going to take her to Greece two days later. I thought we had succeeded. But two weeks later Tiba and her father went back to Heet. The coalition authority had not allowed them to leave. The Greeks didn't have the necessary papers. In the end, I was able to arrange for a Greek military plane to land in Kuwait. But Tiba's condition had gotten so much worse that they refused to take her. Army doctors were able to stabilize her and she could finally leave. When I heard she'd gotten to Greece, that was my best day serving in Iraq. But she died a few days later. We had waited too long. That's my most painful memory. Because, you see, I had the impression that if I could save her, just her, my mission in Iraq would have done some good."

In New York, a soldier's mother had told me about the combat of Ivan Medina, a twenty-two-year-old soldier in the Third Infantry Division. I went to his little house in Middletown, where he told me his story. I wanted to understand how you become an antiwar activist when you're a soldier.

Ivan had just come back from eleven months' service in Iraq when one day he had seen them in the doorway of his little house in Middletown: an officer from West Point and an army chaplain in full uniform, the duo haunting the nightmares of all the families of American soldiers. They were standing there under the American flag, once again bringing the bad news, solemn, in formal uniform as though to dramatize the misfortune. Ivan's twin brother Irving had just been killed by a grenade fired on his convoy in Baghdad. A shell fragment had hit him in the head. Ten hours later he was dead. Ivan told me of his father's tears and the shouts of his mother, who wanted to drive the messengers away. "We received some money from the army: twelve thousand dollars. That's the price of a soldier for the army of the United States," he said bitterly. I was moved seeing his dignified mother taking care of her clean little house. Life had to go on, and yet every day she had before her eyes the living image of her dead son. The walls held pictures of the twins at every stage of their lives, inseparable. But even though he had lost his double, his friend, every window in the house was decorated with an American flag. It was out of love for the country that had welcomed him that Ivan had decided to violate the code that bars soldiers from saying what they think of this war. Besides, since he was the only son in the family still alive, Ivan had been able to leave the army. Despite his timidity and the lisp that troubled him, he jumped in "in the name of all the soldiers who are looking for a way not to go back to Iraq."

All the children in the Medina family, who were from Mexico City, had joined the army "to do something for this country, and above all to pay for college." In Middletown, a little town three hours north of New York, blighted by unemployment and Latino gangs, army recruiters made their pitch right in the schools, promising new recruits a golden future. "One-fourth of my class signed up." Jenny Medina, now twenty-six, had opened the way for her brothers. Things had turned out well for her — she hadn't yet been sent to Iraq. Thanks to her legal training, she had been able to travel around the United States with the army. Ivan and Irving would have preferred to serve in Afghanistan. They had never believed in the war in Iraq. "For me, from the beginning, it was very clear that this was an unjust war that had only two motives: oil and revenge of the Bushes, father and son, against Saddam. My brother and I had the impression that we were being sent to Iraq to settle a family quarrel."

A chaplain's assistant, supposed to be the spiritual guide for four companies of 125 men each in the Third Infantry Division, Ivan told me he had heard hundreds of confessions from frightened young men, traumatized because they had killed: "Kids of eighteen who picked up body parts, who saw their buddies come back in body bags." During the war, on the way from Kuwait to Baghdad, even though he was a chaplain's assistant, Ivan had had to kill men. "I don't feel pity for the fedayeen, it was us or them. But a lot of them didn't want to fight. So of course I keep on thinking about the families waiting for the men we killed, men who will never come back. Like Irving."

I was impressed that he was able to draw the parallel — the war had made him compassionate.

He told me that his worst memory went back to the day Baghdad fell. "We were happy, we'd made good progress. And then there was a missile attack. It was like in the movies, it went very fast and at the same time very gently. Cries, faces, flying body parts."

And then there was Fallujah, where Ivan had served for three months, Fallujah and its "collateral damage." "There are no such things as intelligent bombs. We killed so many innocent people." But what shocked the young man most was the attitude of some NCOs — when they made mistakes, they covered for each other and blamed rank-and-file soldiers.

According to Ivan, improper treatment of prisoners began long before Abu Ghraib. "When we captured Baghdad, some officers took revenge on mere looters. They were bloody and their bodies were covered with bruises. I told the chaplain about it, but at some level the matter was covered up."

Ivan had now decided to campaign against the war in Iraq. "We have to reestablish contact with the international community to try to get something good out of this war that we never should have started."

Ivan was so convincing that after I had visited my soldier friends, I believed that a movement of resisters or of conscientious objectors would grow in the United States. There were so many people traumatized by what they had seen and by the way the situation in Iraq had developed. But Iraq was not Vietnam. It was as though September 11 had paralyzed the capacity of American people to protest against a badly conducted war. As a

Vietnam veteran I met in Iraq explained: "This war is much more politically correct than Vietnam. You remember the dozens of names we gave our Vietnam enemies? Here they're 'the bad guys.' An intangible enemy. An obscure and nameless enemy. Evil incarnate. But suppose in the end those men were not so different from us?"

10

Journey to the Land of Hatred:
Through Iraq from Kuwait to Turkey
March–April 2004

O NE YEAR AFTER THE AMERICAN OFFENSIVE, the photographer Stanley Greene and I made arrangements to travel
through Iraq from Kuwait to the Turkish border. We
wanted to create a travel diary describing daily life in the Iraqi
towns we traveled through, a story not yet covered in the press.
We would therefore try to stay away from coalition bases and
from insurgents so we could see and understand how ordinary
Iraqis were living. In Paris, both the magazine and my family
were urging me to get away from the war. There must be something else, another life, my colleagues said. And my reporting
had become so gloomy they were beginning to think I had an axe
to grind. As for me, I would welcome not hearing the sound of
bullets and grenades, high explosives and deadly missiles.

We decided to leave in the middle of one of the lulls Iraq experienced sporadically, lulls that always filled me with hope and
always ended in disappointment. This time, too, we would soon
be plunged back into the war whether we wanted it or not. Pervasive violence and the armed rebellion of Muqtada al-Sadr's
Shiites demonstrated once again that normality was still an unknown element in Iraq. War had destroyed the once carefree
spirit of the Iraqis. Going through Umm Qasr, Fao, Basra,
Qurna, Nasiriya, and Najaf, towns marking steps in the advance
of American and British assault troops moving north, from the

entry of coalition forces on March 20 to the fall of Baghdad on April 9, 2003, we discovered that one year after Saddam's defeat, real power in Iraq was in the hands of religious extremists and their militias. And now the "liberators" had become the "occupiers," and were falling every day to insurgents' bullets.

This was the first time Stanley Greene had been in Iraq. I was delighted to be going with him. I had been struck dumb by an exhibition of his photographs of the war in Chechnya. He didn't take "beautiful" pictures, he captured the sidelights of horror. The way the people he photographed looked out at you was powerful, overwhelming. I was also aware that our trip would be incredibly dangerous. Stanley had no idea what was involved in crossing Iraq now from end to end in a yellow cab. He was used to risky places, but it would take him some time to realize that in Iraq, danger was ubiquitous and impalpable. His dark complexion made Iraqis take him for an Arab — that is, a terrorist — a mistake that almost cost him his life in Shiite demonstrations where everyone was on the lookout for foreign fighters. People found it hard to believe that he was American. And then there was his earring, a lucky diamond he wouldn't remove regardless of rude remarks that often put us in uncomfortable positions.

Our journey began in Umm Qasr, the first stop on the road from Kuwait to Baghdad. Muhammad had come to pick us up in his yellow Caprice, and we had hired a very fat Iraqi from Basra, Mahmoud, as guide and interpreter. Worn out by our pace, he fell asleep whenever he sat down on a chair. The first image that struck me was a multicolored line of cars winding over more than a kilometer. Once you crossed the border from Kuwait, every gas station on the road to Basra presented a picture of irritated resignation, as drivers often had to wait five hours to fill their tanks. This was the number one complaint we heard against the occupation forces. One year after the war, in an oil-rich country, the fuel shortage was as bad as on the first day of the British and American invasion. In Umm Qasr, an impoverished town of 150,000 where in Saddam's time every street had had a prisoner, a man sentenced to death, or a martyr, the inhabitants chewed over their resentment against the liberators, like betrayed lovers. I couldn't determine whether the gas shortage was tied to a shortage of soldiers to fight corruption and diversion of fuel, the source of the lines. What was obvious was that, one year after the war, people were still faring worse than under the despised dictator. "Last month, there was no milk in the rations. This month, there's no rice, and we still don't have running water." A furious merchant in the souk demanded that I note down the coalition's unmet promises. At the town fountain, children threw stones at us — my *abaya* was new, so they took me for a Kuwaiti. Everyone here detested the neighboring country that lorded it over Iraq. Kuwait with its lofty living standards and its petrodollars had become a scapegoat, made responsible for all the destruction and all the shortages.

In Basra, I made the acquaintance of a remarkable man, one of the heroes of the new Iraq who are prepared to give their lives to rebuild their country. General Qaduum, chief of police in the largest city in southern Iraq, was forty. He belonged to the new generation of cops, and his primary fight was against the fuel smuggling. I asked him to explain the problem. He told me that every day he stopped tanker trucks with dual tanks; instead of distributing fuel to gas stations, they sold it to oil tankers anchored in the Shatt al-Arab halfway between Iraq and Iran. I wondered how it was possible that the coalition had been unable to resolve this crucial symbolic problem, which Iraqis had made into an emblem of the decline in their living standards since the American invasion. Most of the time he was powerless. The smugglers' papers were in order, endorsed by political parties, members of the Iraqi Governing Council. Some of them even bore the signature of the Coalition Provisional Authority, which further stymied him. "Chalabi's Rifah Party, the ally of the Americans, is at the heart of the smuggling in the region," Qaduum asserted. "At least Saddam was alone. Now we have to deal with a hundred Saddams vying for position, and when we ask the British for help, they talk about free trade."

At least once a week, Qaduum patrolled the forty-five ports running from Fao to Basra that exported contraband oil and gasoline, ports that had such suggestive names as al-Flous (Money). Through the same ports came clandestine fighters from Iran suspected of responsibility for several bloody attacks. To show his men he was not afraid, Qaduum drove his car himself at the head of a procession of fifteen armed policemen. He was eager that I understand the magnitude of the smuggling that was corrupting his country. I left Muhammad's taxi and joined him in his car. Without his escort, it would have been impossible for me to go to those squalid ports where a ton of oil went for more than two hundred dollars. All the smugglers were armed, prepared to defend their business vigorously. As I traveled, I discovered that all the little ports presented the same picture — large rusty oil tankers surrounded by swarms of little wooden boats. The opposite shore, a few hundred yards away, was Iran. When we got to Fao, the sun was setting on a gigantic portrait of Khomeini. Before Operation Iraqi Freedom, a photograph of Saddam of the same size had faced it. When they saw us, the smugglers took off in their boats into the reeds. Police pursued them but came back empty-handed, covered in mud up to their waists. It had been a long time since anyone fished here. Fuel never got to the port, and the black market price was too high for fishermen. And yet, all along this extremely sensitive border, we met not a single checkpoint or patrol of coalition forces. At one intersection, a good asphalt road led to the port of Barak. Trucks loaded with new cars without plates, coming from the United Arab Emirates, came out of the huge port, which was guarded like a fortress. But we would go no farther. Barak was the port of Khaled al-Amar, an uncle of Bin Laden himself, Qaduum explained with a sigh. "This is a private port; I don't have the power to enter. They would think I was attacking and would open fire." I couldn't believe my ears.

We headed back to Basra at nightfall. In the darkness, Qaduum gave voice to his pessimistic feelings: "You know, humanity's first crime took place in my country when Cain murdered Abel. Blood has always flowed here. It wasn't Saddam who destroyed my country, it was my people." Rarely did one come across men in authority in Iraq who assumed their share of responsibility for the pervasive disorder. On the road we could see a large lake of black oil: "The punctured pipelines, the ripped-up cables, my people are responsible for them. And when we try to work to improve things, people treat us as spies. I tell them: do you think the Saudis and the Iranians need me? Look around you — they're everywhere, walking around as if they were at home. They don't need spies."

On the road to Basra, burned-out shells of Soviet-made Iraqi army tanks were scattered in the ditches like discarded toys. I knew that getting close to these wrecks posed a serious health risk. But Stanley insisted: ecological catastrophes resulting from war were his obsession. Researchers had measured the radioactivity that the tanks were still emitting from the depleted uranium used in shells that had hit them the year before. The figures were alarming. Children rooted around in the debris around the tanks looking for something to eat. Even if the situation were to improve now, it would be decades before Iraq got over its wars.

In the Basra hospital I met Dr. Jenan Hassan, a remarkable woman, head of the service for children with leukemia. She was expecting an upsurge in child patients in 2005. Before Operation Desert Storm, there had been only nineteen children with leukemia each year. But in the last few years she had been taking in more than two hundred per year. There has been a good deal of talk in the West about Gulf War Syndrome, less about the fatal repercussions of the war on the Iraqis. Not to mention all the children whose parents were not rich enough to send them to Baghdad for treatment. Wearing a turquoise *hijab*, the energetic forty-seven-year-old doctor went on her rounds. Since the fall of the regime, the rate of cure in her service had increased from 20 to 50 percent, thanks to an Austrian NGO that had taken charge of the wing for children with leukemia. But when she talked about the atmosphere in the city, the pediatrician lost her buoyant optimism. "Before, I could make a run to the hospital at two in the morning. Now my colleagues are being assassinated one after the other. We have one hundred sixty political parties in Basra. New pictures have replaced the old ones, but I don't see any difference."

Dr. Hassan's children went to school with bodyguards, and her daughter, harassed by Islamists trying to indoctrinate her, had stopped attending the university. A few weeks earlier, one of the Islamist parties had tried to take over the hospital, but the energetic doctor had driven off the militia. "Since then, we have been making rounds to defend our hospital. But how long can we hold out?"

The day before we got to Basra, two young women working for the Halliburton subsidiary KBR had been assassinated in the taxi supposed to take them home. Islamist groups claimed responsibility for the crime. "There are parties that have decreed that women should not work for foreigners, or in fact for anyone," explained the police chief. That was another aspect of the reality of the new Iraq. Women were the ones who had gained the least from the change of regime. I couldn't stop wondering as I traveled around Iraq why the Americans had not ensured that women were guaranteed their basic rights. Women were now afraid that a law would be promulgated requiring all women to be veiled as in Iran. As was always the case here, the rights of women were sacrificed on the altar of politics, and carried little weight compared to the challenges represented by the possible partition of the country and the distribution of oil resources.

I recalled a terrible scene I had witnessed the night of the attack that cost Ayatollah al-Hakim his life. A mother was looking for the body of her child. By lifting sheets in the morgue, she had managed to put together the grim jigsaw puzzle of the dispersed parts of her child's body. Then, with the men of her family, she headed for one of the mausoleums in the Najaf cemetery. But at the door to the mortuary, a cleric with a black turban had driven off the grief-stricken mother with a click of the tongue: "No women here, it's holy."

"Barred to women," "Close your *abaya*," "Cover your hair": in Iraq since the fall of Saddam's regime, instructions have rained down on women. Among the Shiites in particular, I have noticed that restored community pride demands strict respect for sexual discrimination. You have to have been cloaked in an *abaya*, un-recognizable, and chased away from some religious bureau with a flick of a hand to understand how women are seen in the holy city. Western women have a particular status in the country — not really women but employers, hybrid beings, economic enti-ties, or at worst prostitutes.

Merely by taking a tour through the Basra prison, you could understand the harsh reality of women's life in Iraq at the time. In this squalid prison reeking of urine, 350 prisoners were piled into six cells. In the women's section, there were just eleven pris-oners. Even the guard admitted that only one of them really de-served to be in jail. Iman Abdallah, thirty-three, had thrown a grenade at an official building in exchange for a few dollars. She was an orphan and had justified her act by her poverty, knowing that she would probably spend the rest of her life in prison. For the others, it was a different story.

To enable me to speak to her, they let Asil Jaseem out of prison. This very pretty eighteen-year-old with brown hair had been kidnapped and raped. The police had picked her up, and a judge had put her in prison so that her family would not be tempted to kill her to restore its honor. She had now been in pro-tective custody for three months. The guard had few illusions about what awaited her: as soon as she was released, she would be killed.

Dunia Abdul Wahad was accused of murder. In fact, her brother had killed a man who had been harassing her. But be-cause she was "the cause" of the crime, she would have to pay the penalty. She had been in prison for five months and ten days. Her cellmate was a retarded woman. Next came a fifteen-year-old girl, the pretty sister of a kidnapper who had escaped arrest;

she was serving a sentence in his place. Tortured by these innocent women's plight and my inability to change or help, I left the
prison in a state of fury and despair.

On the road to Nasiriya lies the town of Suq al-Shuyukh, a
few hundred houses bordering a dusty street leading to the railroad tracks. This town was driving Colonel Luigi Scollo, the
Italian officer, at the head of Task Force 11 in charge of the region, to distraction. Sharing a glass of wine (the Italians were the
only soldiers allowed to drink), the colonel described this accursed town where Shiite extremists ran the show. The specialty
of Suq al-Shuyukh was attacking the train from Basra to Baghdad. It was said that the bandits had an understanding with the
driver, who would slow down when he approached the little
town. Passengers brave or reckless enough to travel on the ghost
train, most of whose windows were broken, were few and far between.

As Stanley soon discovered, this was not the only thing
wrong with Suq al-Shuyukh. A short distance from the railroad
tracks, the ecological disaster of the town's sewers could be seen.
Torrents of contaminated white foam were pouring directly into
the river from which some people drew their "potable" water.
The vision of this devastation was overwhelming. Despite the
growing crowd of children who were beginning to jostle us, and
ignoring the warnings of Mahmoud and Muhammad, both of
whom were becoming visibly afraid, Stanley took his time pho-
tographing the white foam.

When we finally managed to persuade him to leave town, a
pickup truck full of Iraqi policemen came out of nowhere and
blocked the road. A dozen Kalashnikovs were trained on us, and
we held our breath. In this town, the inhabitants really believed
that the attacks devastating the country were the work of Americans wanting to justify their presence in Iraq. We had been
taken for American terrorists. The townspeople had called Baghdad and the local police. A strand of blond hair peeking out from
my scarf and Stanley's earring had drawn suspicion on us. We ex-

plained ourselves without getting out of the car, keeping our hands in full view.

Once the "misunderstanding" had been cleared up, the police asked us to follow them. But a car soon came between us, carrying members of the militia of Muqtada al-Sadr's Shiite extremist party with their fingers on the triggers. They stopped us and listened to our defense, while the Iraqi police respectfully withdrew.

"Do you know that you almost died?" scolded Adnan Dawi, a representative from al-Sadr's office who had been told of our presence by the local militia. "Have you forgotten that you have to register with local authorities in every town?" Seeing the deference shown by the local people to Dawi, I quickly understood he represented the authorities in question.

When I had spoken to specialists on Iraq's political figures, everyone had agreed that Muqtada was a mere agitator who had no real power. My trip through the south totally contradicted their view. I realized that this champion of the disinherited had outposts everywhere, a social network that reminded me of the one Islamists had established in Algeria.

Traumatized by an attack that had cost the lives of sixteen of their soldiers in November 2003, the Italians had withdrawn to the Nasiriya airport. The base carried reminders of the Italy I loved. There was the wine, the soldiers' accent, and the coffee, as good as in Italy, that they were always drinking at night before going out on patrol.

That day they were leaving one of their last positions in the town, the museum of Nasiriya. Mr. Hamdani, the director, at first refused to show me around his museum, claiming he didn't have the necessary permits. After a good deal of discussion I understood that the real problem was that he was ashamed of what he had to show me. When he finally agreed to let me visit his establishment, I saw the reasons for the reluctance of this cultivated man: wine bottles on the bases of statues of Sumerian gods, plastic scattered on the floor, and remains of meals. In the face of this disheartening spectacle, the archaeologist was unable to hold back his tears. Overcome in turn, Stanley embraced him. In the little room where he had stored the treasures from Sumerian sites, he let us touch cuneiform tablets and five-thousand-year-old children's toys. I was deeply moved by his passion, and shared his obvious distress.

With an escort of fifteen customs agents, we went with him to the site of the earliest known Mesopotamian temple, the palace of Gudaia, about fifty miles from Nasiriya. Forty statues exhibited in the Louvre come from this site. But it now looked as though an army had plowed up the earth. Looters in the pay of Baghdad antiquities dealers, themselves supplying their Western counterparts, had systematically dug up, ravaged, reduced to dust this fabulous storehouse of ancient history. Since Islamist sheikhs had given their blessing to the looters if they agreed to give the mosque 20 percent of their earnings, the hunt for antiquities had been open. Baghdad merchants could, for a few dollars, get their hands on pottery and cuneiform tablets sought after by Western collectors. Little effort was required. All they had to do was skim the sea of Mesopotamian potsherds, without even having to dig, to pick up cuneiform tablets, royal seals, and small bas-reliefs.

A bit farther on, in Umma, where I tripped over intact Sumerian vases dating from 2500 BC, robbers had destroyed a large part of the walls of the ancient city. The market was now saturated with pieces from that period, and Western dealers were looking for objects more than five thousand years old. Looters were destroying everything found above the oldest layers. "For collectors, those pieces are only more pretty pottery for their display cases," Hamdani lamented. "For us, it's the missing link allowing us to decipher the first civilization in the world." I was ashamed as I recalled the statuette I had bought from an antique dealer in Paris. To defend this cradle of humanity against the looters, there was only a nearly blind old man who used his

Kalashnikov as a cane. There was no trace of the Italian cara-
binieri in black uniforms armed like characters in a science fic-
tion movie who patrolled the streets of Nasiriya in their armored
vehicles, even though they presumably were in charge of protecting these sites.

In the courthouse of the city of Najaf in the office of the chief
judge, I met twenty judges sunk deep in their armchairs. Not a
single woman, I noted — the last one who with the protection of
the Americans had tried to get appointed had had to give up in
the face of opposition from the entire population of the city. In
any event, there was no work to be had, so the middle-aged
judges were all sipping tea. With nothing else to do, they had the
time to count up their assassinated colleagues. There was, of
course, the former chief judge of Najaf, the judge in Mosul, the
one in Kirkuk, and recently the one in Hilla. There were no
hearings, no routine divorces, nothing. After the fall of the despised regime, people could finally turn to religious authorities
or tribal sheikhs to settle their differences.

The most popular of these new "centers of sharia law" was
that of Muqtada al-Sadr. In a narrow alley, a dense crowd was
gathered outside the headquarters of the champion of the disinherited of Najaf. From beneath their black turbans, the men cast
looks of hatred at me, because I bore the dual curse of being a
foreigner and a woman. They were all waiting only for a sign
from the guide to take up arms against the invader. In the end
they let us come in. We had to lower our eyes, avoid meeting the
looks of petitioners filled with hostility to foreigners. I had gotten used to this open hatred that greeted me at every street corner in the city.

In the small hearing rooms in Muqtada's court, both judges
and parties squatted on the cement floor. In this "legal tribunal,"
sharia was being applied completely illegally, with no intervention or criticism from the American forces. Eighteen months before the constituent assembly, sharia was in fact being applied in

the most important holy city in Iraq. The "tribunal," which was open only in the morning, handled more than fifty cases a day. No diploma was required to be a judge: one only had to have sufficiently studied the Koran. The building even had a small prison. Everything was done to reconcile the disputants. If a complainant refused any form of compensation and the "judge" found the accused guilty, the injured parties themselves carried out the sentences, cut off the hands of thieves, and executed murderers. Most of the time, however, the parties agreed to financial compensation. We sat cross-legged next to a handsome, levelheaded, and attentive man of about thirty, Sheikh Ahmed al-Hussein, who was judging, as he listened to the weeping parties, a dispute over an inheritance between two brothers. It was paradoxical, but clearly the population preferred this form of justice to that dispensed by the court of Najaf. The judges were more human than the "real" judges, who were formal, somber, and distant. And things went much more quickly. A young man accompanied by two old men accused his great-uncle, who was there, of having killed his grandfather in 1961; he had a tape on which the guilty man confessed his crime. Judgment was rendered in twenty minutes — the old man was let off with a fine. And social and religious pressure was strong enough for the sentence to be applied without discussion. When necessary, the police collaborated with the "legal" tribunal. "They even helped us arrest the alcohol sellers who refused to come before us," Sheikh Ahmed acknowledged with satisfaction.

This Islamic justice, which had had such a regressive effect on the situation of Iraqi women, was shocking, but it was not hard to understand that people came to these courts looking for some of the humanity that could not be found in the stiff-necked judges of the old regime. I remembered a judge in Baghdad who had sentenced two thieves to life in prison as their lawyer's labored and incoherent argument was inaudible even to the judge. In the end, the hearing had been interrupted by gunfire and everyone in the courtroom had dispersed, including the police who were supposed to guard the prisoners.

*   *   *

When we finally reached Baghdad, the first thing I noticed, the most spectacular change from my earlier visits, was the frenzied pace of consumption, the rage to buy. After traveling through the poverty-stricken south, Baghdad felt like New York. On the sidewalks of fashionable neighborhoods like Arasat and al-Mansur, mountains of boxes of consumer goods were overflowing. You could find television sets for less than $100, satellite dishes for $75, washing machines for $150, about a month's salary for a government employee. I found myself beginning to hope again. Suppose the militias and Shiite fanaticism had won only in the south, and in the capital economic recovery could guarantee some degree of stability. I wanted to believe. Even mobile phones had reached this forsaken city. The stores where you bought them were air-conditioned, with affable sales personnel using the same enthusiastic slogans as their Western counterparts. And yet, when we left the store, my translator asked me to walk ten yards in front of him; he was afraid of being the target of gunfire, and I realized that, even at this time, in Baghdad there were still problems.

But in Baghdad, Iraqis, or at least the men, could breathe a little between attacks. In the evening there were lines in front of al-Faqma, the best ice cream seller in the city, and on the banks of the Tigris, for the first time since the war, the domino players had returned to their old positions in al-Beiruti. On the terrace of this old Baghdad café, where the waiters wore red vests, the March breeze carried the pleasant scent of the river. A boat glided on the water, and the image of prewar Baghdad flashed before my eyes. But the illusion of peace never lasted long. According to Iraqi police, there were still about twenty-five attacks every day in the capital. I tried to find out how the inhabitants of Baghdad relaxed, what they did in their free time. Almost all the movie theaters had closed under pressure from religious fundamentalists. In a Baghdad suburb I finally came on a shabby café where secret cockfights were held. In the filthy back room there was a little ring covered with feathers and blood. Men were sipping soda and yelling out their bets while cocks named Osama and Saddam tore each other apart. It was sordid and it smelled bad, but there was relief in seeing something other than war. It was there, in that dirty back room, that I recognized for the first time what I had come to Iraq to see: Iraqis carrying on in spite of everything.

In Baghdad on Friday, the day of prayer, tanks and armed militias took up positions in front of "sensitive" mosques. Ibrahim, a fourteen-year-old in a sweat suit, the son of a friend, was on duty at his neighborhood mosque. Although he tried to look detached, you could sense that he was proud to show off with his Kalashnikov in front of his jealous friends. A few days earlier, the newly constructed Shiite mosque in the neighborhood had been destroyed by a bomb. In the logic of reprisal, one of the Salafist notables in the neighborhood had been assassinated, and then the Sunni mosque was attacked. Tension was so high that armed bodyguards accompanied the sheikh inside the mosque, sacrilege for a Muslim. But the still latent conflict between Shiites and Sunnis was not the subject of the sheikh's sermon that day.

To hear the sermon, I persuaded with some difficulty the wife of a friend to go with me to the women's section upstairs. It was empty — Iraqi women prayed at home, out of sight. Through the *musharabiya*, intended to keep us from being seen, I observed the sheikh, draped in his roomy white tunic over which flowed his long black beard, get carried away with emotion against the "invader." He compared the good aroma that came from the bodies of martyrs with the pestilential smell emanating from American corpses. His sermon was maudlin and repetitive. After a half hour I started to drift off, hypnotized by his monotonous rhythm. "We are all going to die, that is our fate as men," the sheikh prophesied tearfully. "Then let us die bravely. Let us imitate the example of Sheikh Yassin* and the martyrs who blow themselves up in car bombs in Israel." How many would have the

---

* The spiritual guide of the Palestinian Hamas Party, assassinated by the Israeli army on March 22, 2004.

strength to resist the argument? The worshippers in the mosque, several of whom I knew, had all been won over by this warrior catechism. But few of them would act on it.

I continued my journey north. I was in Kirkuk when I learned that the revolt of Muqtada al-Sadr's supporters, which I had felt taking shape throughout my long trip through the south, was in the process of breaking out in Iraq in earnest. I was angry at myself for having allowed myself to hope. There had already been too many disputes, divisions, and mistakes to escape from the inevitable spiral of war. For the anniversary of the capture of Baghdad by the coalition forces, the marines were anticipating an attack by Saddam's supporters or the Sunnis who had been left out of the new Iraq. But the revolt came from the disciples of the young Shiite extremist who preached obligatory wearing of the long black *abaya* by women and the prohibition of music, dancing, and above all alcohol. It was the closing of a newspaper, *al-Hawza*, followed by the arrest of one of the young cleric's lieutenants, that had unleashed the insurrection. A few days before his arrest by the coalition forces, I had interviewed this spokesman for Muqtada, Mustapha Ali al-Yacubi. We had spoken about Chechnya. He had given Stanley and me one of his rings, which we would use as a safe-conduct pass among his supporters during the revolt. Al-Yacubi had forcefully demanded the withdrawal of Americans from Iraq, comparing their presence in the country to the German occupation of France, but he also asserted that the time for his followers to revolt had not yet come. It was his arrest that had changed the minds of his supporters. They had been right to understand it as a declaration of war by the Americans, determined to get rid of the Shiite agitator and of the sanctuary of Fallujah before the coming legislative elections.

I decided to go to the mosque used as headquarters by Muqtada's group in Kirkuk. A crowd had assembled at the entrance to the holy place. Tension was high. After a good deal of discussion, the translator I had hired in Baghdad, a man named Mazen, and I were authorized to enter the patio of the mosque after being thoroughly searched. Mazen was very afraid of Shiite fanaticism, and his expression showed it. I always made fun of him and tweaked him because he began all his sentences, "Honestly speaking." This time he was true to form: "Honestly speaking, Sara, I think these people will kill us."

In the courtyard, the first person I spoke to was an extremely agitated man who accused me of belonging to the CIA and flourished a revolver in my face. I had asked Stanley to wait for me in the car because he was American. I was glad I'd had that reflex and hoped he wouldn't get tired of waiting and try to barge in. The man spoke in disjointed sentences. Finally he said: "You're talking to a dead man." Ali, a thirty-year-old computer programmer, had decided to become a suicide bomber. He explained that it was the most important decision in his life: in a few hours, for the sake of his leader Muqtada, who was being hunted down by the Americans, he would blow himself up in front of the target assigned to him. He railed against the Kurds, the Americans' "dogs." Then he took his head in his hands. "I hate the war," he sighed. His eyes wandered, his voice grew softer. His voice full of tears, he told me how he had said goodbye to his mother that morning. "I do not like to fight, but the hour of sacrifice has come. I dreamed of a quiet little life. A room in my father's house that I would have shared with a wife who would have argued with my mother. Kids. But the order has come and I am going to die." He stopped, stricken, in the middle of a sentence, remained silent for a few minutes, and then went on: "We Shiites are used to living with tragedy and martyrdom. We are all prepared to die, but we will sell our lives dear."

I listened to this profession of faith I had heard so many times before but had never been able to understand. How could you do yourself in for a leader or a cause? There was such a contradiction between the strength of the political commitment and the nihilism of suicide. The discipline and supernatural faith of these people fascinated me.

When we got back to Baghdad, we found a small group of frustrated reporters in the Hotel al-Hamra. It was impossible to go to Fallujah, which was surrounded by the American army, and it was very dangerous to cover the Shiite revolt. The practice of kidnapping was in its early stages, and nearly forty foreigners from at least twelve different countries were being held hostage. Some of them, Japanese, Czechs, Italians, and Americans, came from countries with troops in Iraq, and the armed groups holding them threatened to execute them unless their governments withdrew their forces. I and the other Western reporters were excluded from the two fronts in the war, because in the month of April 2004 we had become one of the targets in this confrontation between Islam and the West.

The gap between Western and Arab reporters was increasing. It seemed to be necessary to choose sides, to defend the vision of the world held by one's own people. Sihem Bensedrin, a Tunisian reporter and opposition figure who had come to Baghdad to train Iraqi reporters, described to me the violent reaction of her colleagues against what she was doing. She was guilty of going to a country occupied by Americans, of ratifying the occupation by her presence. For some Arab reporters, once the war had begun, it became as reprehensible to go to Iraq as to go to Israel.

At the same time, the American government had begun to trust only "its own" and the English reporters. French reporters, with few illusions, went back and forth between the two sides in the war and the two press camps.

I decided to leave the hotel, where we were going mad from idleness. The battle between Muqtada's supporters and American soldiers was about to break out in Najaf. Stanley and I decided it was safer for me to go there alone with Muhammad. There were frequent insurgent checkpoints on the road, but sitting next to Muhammad in his yellow Caprice wearing a long *abaya*, I could pass for one of his relatives. We set out early in the morning in order to be able to start back from the holy city before the nightly curfew.

The first thing I noticed in Najaf, as we approached the mausoleum of Imam Ali, was the silence. Omar, whom I'd met at the home of Ayatollah Muhammad Baqir al-Hakim the day before his assassination, had been my guide in the city since the death of his leader. This time he was reluctant to accompany me in my walk around Ali's mosque even though I was covered from head to foot by my *abaya*.

Usually, my manner of walking immediately gave me away. I didn't walk with my head bent and my eyes lowered as a sign of submission, like a local woman. Sometimes, to compel my inter-locutors to answer, I even looked them in the eye and spoke loudly to counteract the effect of the *abaya*, a sign of submission to their power. But this time I played the game, taking small steps and keeping my head lowered to avoid being unmasked. In spite of the blinding sunlight, I had taken off my sunglasses. At worst, I would be taken for an Iranian on pilgrimage.

It felt as though we were at a wake. All that could be heard was the wind flapping the women's *abayas* and sometimes the beeps of the detection devices screening worshippers entering the mosque. The combination of weapons and faith reminded me of the Wailing Wall. The whole city was whispering. Residents barricaded in their houses were holding their breath. Ayatollah al-Sistani's street was blocked off by a large black cloth. Dozens of men in black were standing guard in front of Muq-tada's office. At every street corner, militiamen in the "Mahdi Army," armed with grenade launchers and Kalashnikovs, were pacing up and down or playing cards. Everyone was scrutinizing everyone else, as though we were on a western set in a medieval city, trying to determine who would strike first. Omar was terri-fied. Every few minutes, he whispered to me: "You don't know them; if they find us out, they'll kill us." I thought about the CIA agent I'd met in the palace who had been paraded around the streets of Fallujah pretending he was mute. It was intoxicating — a black ghost, I walked through the streets of this silent city elec-tric with tension that might explode into battle at any moment.

Before going back to Baghdad, I went to see Sheikh Muham-mad, a spokesman for Ayatollah al-Sistani, whom the Americans were still presenting as a moderate. Muhammad had taken refuge in his house. He defended the motives of the young extremist who had launched the revolt, even though he didn't like him. The radical tone of his language astonished me. What if the Americans were fostering another Khomeini? He explained his distrust of the Americans: "They are obsessed with weakening the Shiites so they can turn over control of the country to their Iraqi agents." According to this professor of philosophy in the Hawza of Najaf, after Muqtada the next American target was the Badr Brigade, aware of the threat it was under. But what stoked Sheikh Mohammed's rage against the Americans was their refusal to provide for the application of sharia in the constitution: "Don't you understand that the American invasion was driven by ideological and cultural motives? They want to influence our laws and prevent us from applying the Koran, just like Saddam. But with or without Muqtada, the Shiites' patience is at an end. Islam is now under attack and jihad is on the march. Iran has been corrupted by the West. You'll see: one day Iraq will be the first true Islamic republic," explained the spokesman of the Americans' so-called ally in Iraq.

11

The Barbarity of Fallujah
April 2004

ONE MORNING BETWEEN ASSIGNMENTS, Stanley and I were sunning ourselves on the front steps of the Hotel al-Hamra in Baghdad. I liked to sit there, even though we had been strongly advised against lingering in the area. I liked to watch the spectacle of private security men, tough guys getting out of their SUVs, bow-legged, with their hands on their guns like cowboys. The handkerchief seller, a deaf-mute who made hostile gestures toward reporters who didn't give her a coin, was at her post. The businessmen wearing Stetsons, drinking whiskey, delighted with the deals they'd made at the end of the war, had deserted this hotel in favor of the Palestine or the Sheraton in the Green Zone. The only people left were bodyguards, some mysterious people suspected of being CIA agents, and us, the reporters.

I had just sent in my article describing our month-and-a-half traversal of Iraq. That night I also had to write an article about the revolt of the Shiites, which was growing in the south and in Baghdad. I had the impression that I was free for a few hours. In Iraq, moments of respite had to be taken when you could find them. I closed my eyes, paying no attention to the muffled sounds and the gunshots scattered around the city. For a moment, I was impervious to the violence that had engulfed me in the course of the last few weeks. With so many events, so many attacks, overwhelming one's mind, the natural reflex was to conserve resources whenever one could. The spring sun warmed us gently. Stanley and I were talking with the translators who always gravitated around the hotel looking for a job that wouldn't be too dangerous. Since my incursions into insurgent territory, I felt like a tainted woman, for most were no longer eager to work with me. They had even taken to calling Stanley and me the kamikazes. We had gone through six translators in a month. They rightly felt increasingly threatened since the beginning of the Shiite revolt, and imposed ever greater restrictions before agreeing to work with us.

Suddenly a man drove up in front of the hotel, crying and shouting, and taking his head in his hands. He had just witnessed a terrible scene in Fallujah, still the capital of resistance to the American occupation. Through his sobs, he described the savagery of an angry crowd, a primitive lynching that chilled us to the bone. Four American contractors had been burned alive, and the residents were now dragging their bodies through the city. Stanley was horrified but, true to his photographer's instincts, asked me if we could go there.

I hesitated. I knew that Muhammad would drive me to hell if I asked him. But I had already experienced the violence of the inhabitants of Fallujah, which now had to be boiling over, intoxicated as they must be with the crime they had just committed. Stanley was American, a citizen of the enemy nation, and it was really dangerous. The man told us that American soldiers had stopped him on his way out of Fallujah to ask him for information. By now, there must be a checkpoint and an operation under way to recover the bodies. Stanley suggested that we go to the outskirts of the city to collect information from the marines. We took along as our translator a marvelous man of about fifty who was incredibly courageous. Not only did he have a clubfoot, which gave him some pain, but he was a Shiite, hence detested by the Sunni fanatics of Fallujah.

After an hour's drive, as we were going down a street bordered by dirty concrete houses, Stanley asked if we were approaching the suburbs of Fallujah.

Emerging from my trance, I realized to my surprise and concern that we were already in the center of the city. On our trip there, we had not come across a single American soldier. A few yards in front of us, the shells of two cars were burning, surrounded by a crowd. They were so absorbed by the show that no one was paying any attention to us. Stanley asked a young man to point us to the bridge where we had been told the bodies had finally been hanged. I invited the young man to join us in the car, thinking it would be much safer to have a local citizen with us, and to our surprise he accepted. Abdulkader, who was twenty, told us he had witnessed the scene. According to him, two jeeps driven by American civilians wearing bulletproof vests had been attacked by the "resistance" with RPG-7 grenade launchers. Two of the passengers had survived the impact and tried to climb out of one vehicle, but the inhabitants had driven them back into the flames with shovels and pitchforks. "They were begging, 'Please, please, help!'" he said. I asked him if he had tried to help them. Abdulkader looked at me wide-eyed, as though he didn't even understand my question. "Help Americans?" he said indignantly, looking at me with a mixture of disgust and suspicion.

We approached the little iron bridge. There was another crowd. On the ground I could see a shapeless charred mass. At first I didn't understand what I was seeing. I had not expected to see burned bodies. I was face to face with something incomprehensible, witnessing an unbearable spectacle, in the presence of the very essence of barbarity. We got out of the car. The bodies had been taken down from the bridge, and young men were looking at the charred remains. It seemed as though the flames had forever fixed their terrible agony. I could distinguish an arm that seemed to have been raised in an attempt to provide protection, a fragment of a foot. The flames had caused the bodies to shrivel, and Stanley wondered whether he was looking at a woman. You could see a scrap of red cloth, maybe a belt. Chanting quietly, the men encircling the bodies kicked them and hacked at them with knives. They were not hysterical, and there was no sign of craziness; they seemed content. One of them, holding the handlebars of a bicycle, gave a wide-eyed smile; another was wearing a Malcolm X T-shirt. I had pictured them howling in anger; it was the calm that was terrible. The young men had in fact caught sight of us, and the atmosphere immediately became more tense. I called out to Muhammad, who had wandered away from the car. He later criticized me for shouting. "Don't you know those people are Sunnis like me?" he remonstrated. In Fallujah that day, there was no longer any tribal solidarity, family circle, or clan solidarity that could hold. In this moment of pure animality, if the crowd had turned against us, nothing and no one could have helped us. We beat a hasty retreat to the car; we had not been there ten minutes.

Less than a mile farther on toward the mosque, the shells of the two cars belonging to the Blackwater contractors were still burning. We stopped so I could ask some questions. The crowd were brandishing pictures of the spiritual leader of Hamas, Sheikh Yassin, who had just been assassinated, and chanting slogans that were not exactly welcoming: "Fallujah is the graveyard of Americans" and "We'll cut off the hands of all foreigners."

The circle of revolt was complete: Malcolm X, Palestine, Fallujah, were all jumbled together in the minds of the desperate men of Islam. Was the act so abominable that more than one reason had to be found after the fact to justify the unjustifiable? Was this the explanation for lumping together the American occupation, the assassination of Sheikh Yassin, and the oppression of blacks in America? There were no reasons for this abomination. Their revenge against the infidels?

I looked up and saw, hanging on an electric wire by a thread, a leg that had been cut off at the femur. As a photographer, Stanley had recorded many more macabre details than I, and even he burst into tears of disgust.

We were the only Westerners who had been in Fallujah that day. The images I saw then have since been confused in my mind with photographs of the scene I saw afterward. I don't think the leg hanging by a thread was ever photographed, but I remember the photograph, not the actual scene. My most horrible, vivid memory is the odor of burned flesh, and for that I have been unable to devise a filter.

How did we manage to get out of Fallujah alive? I was shielded by the folds of my *abaya*, and Stanley's dark complexion made it easy to mistake him for an Arab reporter, so no one suspected our nationalities. Besides, no one could have imagined that two Westerners would have been reckless enough to venture into a city so crazed by hatred that the crowd would mutilate corpses.

On the way back, my anxiety made me wonder suddenly about my own status. How could I give meaning to what I had just seen? How? What did this barbarity signify? Of course, it had been too late to save the men's lives, but I felt dirtied by the knife blows I had seen inflicted on the charred bodies. I often think of what the men burned alive went through, their pleas for mercy, the indifference of the crowd, the joyful cries of the killers — and of myself, in the midst of that crowd a few hours later.

The corpses spread out before us represented a culmination of our travels through Iraq, a point of no return, and the symbol of a stalemate in any dialogue between Americans and Iraqis. Was that the day when the "resistance" became "terrorists"? When American soldiers began to mistreat a people they had come to "liberate"?

I understood that day that we had reached a turning point in the war. The American soldiers would not leave this act of defiance unpunished. And yet, to our astonishment, two days after the killing and mutilation, there were no helicopters and no tanks in view in Fallujah. The insurgents must have felt great delight when they saw that a patrol had not come to recover the bodies of their fellow citizens. It was during the long interval in which the armed forces had deserted the city that we understood the reprisals would be terrible. The American army was preparing for battle. Iraq had entered into a war of symbols. There was an epic aspect to the barbarity, as with Achilles killing Hector before the ramparts of Troy and dragging the body behind his chariot. The episode in Fallujah was the starting point of the era of icons of the war — the quasi-religious photographs of Christ-like victims, like the masked prisoner of Abu Ghraib and Nicholas Berg on his knees before his executioners.

I needed to speak about what I had seen, and I called my editor, René Backmann, as soon as I got back to Baghdad. A former foreign correspondent who had covered many conflicts and knew how to support people on the ground, he listened attentively and with compassion as I related my story. I also called the people at the Agence France-Presse, then Yan. But before I had got very far he stopped me, horrified. He didn't want to hear the story, and he was afraid he wouldn't be able to continue to reassure my parents and my friends regarding my safety if I gave him any more details. I understood and moved on to another subject.

A few days later, as I had expected, the siege of Fallujah began. We could no longer go to the city unless embedded with a marine unit. The mujahideen in Fallujah were even shooting the Salafist preachers who had cameras, taking them for spies. The Islamic party headquarters had been bombed because it had tried to initiate negotiations with the Americans. And while all this was going on, the whole country was ablaze. There was fighting in Najaf, in Karbala, in the south in Nasiriya. To think that only a few days earlier I had found Baghdad rather calm. There, Muqtada's supporters were starting to take reporters hostage.

Stanley and I made the rounds of the aid agencies to try to find a way to get to Fallujah. But even ambulances of the Red Crescent had been forced to turn back. Several refugee families who had fled the city told us they had been fired on — and some of their relatives killed — by American snipers posted on rooftops. It was the same tragic story from everyone: the streets of Fallujah were littered with corpses, women and children shot in the head as they tried to flee. American soldiers were so afraid of this city, which they thought of as the lair of the forces of evil, that they shot at anything that moved, including dogs.

The horror was escalating, and the wounded were crowding into the hospitals. It was very difficult to find out where they were being treated. The Salafists in Baghdad were hiding them to keep them from being arrested by the Americans. I finally found some of the wounded in Saddam Hospital in Medical City in Baghdad. Stanley's camera was concealed in the folds of my *abaya*. I saw mutilated bodies in their death throes. And then there were the children. In one bed I saw Muhammad Numu-vavy, a twelve-year-old boy, who had lost a leg when his house in the Jawlan neighborhood of Fallujah had been hit by cluster bombs. He didn't know it yet, but his other leg, which had gangrene, would also have to be amputated. Nor did he know that the twenty-four members of his family — brothers, sisters, parents, grandparents, uncles, and cousins — who lived with him in Fallujah had all been killed. The doctors had not yet dared tell him. Oddly, the magnitude of the figure numbed my feelings. I tried to picture the faces of twenty-four of my friends or family members, and I imagined the depths of my despair if they were all to disappear at once. So many things were like that in Iraq: despair, the bleakness of lives, the constant threat of death, often made commiseration impossible.

In the next hospital room I met Asla, who had had to flee with her daughter Intesar and her eighteen-month-old son Huday when her house in the Askari neighborhood had been struck by tank fire. She had been hit by a sniper as she was running in the alley next to her house.

Next to them was a three-year-old boy, sitting on his bed in dead silence. He had lost an eye, and shell fragments were lodged in his skull. One of his hands had been blown off by an explosion. His entire family had disappeared, except for one of his uncles, a forty-five-year-old man who was gently rocking him before my eyes, a man who was to be arrested a few hours later by the coalition forces. Being confronted each day with such indescribable tragedy, I had long ago tried to force myself not to yield to my emotions, in order simply to be able to continue reporting facts, but it was becoming harder with each passing day.

An American magazine had laid out a page of Stanley's photographs depicting the children in the hospital and was ready to go to press, but then decided finally that they were too "graphic," like the pictures of the charred bodies next to the little bridge. One of them, a small picture of Muhammad Numuvavy, was published in *Le Nouvel Observateur* in France, but even my own magazine felt the rest were too devastating to print. Stanley and I felt terribly frustrated. What justification did we have as journalists for being in this stricken land if we couldn't publish what we had seen? We had been hired to tell the story of the war, but no one wanted to know what was really going on here — they preferred pictures and stories of a sanitized, watered-down conflict. Why had we been living in hell if we could not portray it accurately?

It was at that point that, perhaps for the first time, I really understood the feelings of powerlessness and injustice that Iraqis who hated the occupation must have experienced. I felt their rebellion, but to sympathize it is necessary to identify with the suffering of others. Salam, whom I met in Baghdad, was the medium of my identification. Because he was young, ambitious, and cultivated, with a sharp sense of humor in spite of the circumstances, because he reminded me of friends, his suffering and his stories touched me personally, more than any others.

The first time I saw Dr. Salam was in the entrance of the Abu Hanifa mosque in Baghdad, a mosque that had always been a nerve center of resistance to the American occupation. It was here that Saddam Hussein had sought refuge during the early days of the war. That day, I had come to attend prayer in the courtyard of the mosque. Supporters of the Shiite extremist Muqtada al-Sadr were supposed to cross the bridge between the Shiite quarter and this Sunni bastion to pray with their "brothers" against the "invaders" of Fallujah. Rival forces united against the invader — this was a first, and I wanted to be there.

In the large, packed room where the faithful crowded together to contribute their gifts to the Fallujah refugees, I saw this young doctor with burning eyes and drawn features. Exhausted and distraught, Dr. Salam had come in search of blood and medicine. At twenty-eight, this young doctor was one of the most brilliant Iraqi surgeons of his generation. He had just come from besieged Fallujah and was going right back. Our friendship began during the siege. He needed to talk to someone who understood, who listened. For a week, he called me every three hours to recount what was happening in his native city. Then we met again in Baghdad, and later several times in London.

Salam needed to speak about what he had seen in Fallujah. That day at the mosque, I went to hear him. Delivered in a monotone, his speech was very moving. When we came out of the mosque, all the people who had been listening were in tears, including me. My own tears surprised the armed sentinels keeping watch on the roof of the mosque for an assault by the American troops they had been told was coming. "Who hurt you?" asked distressed mujahideen, who came scampering down from the roof (rattling their missile launchers in the process). "Who has brought you to tears?" That day, many men found their calling as "martyrs" in the corner of the mosque listening to Salam.

Dr. Salam described the corpses on the sidewalks. The day before our meeting, he had retrieved more than ten bodies shot with a bullet in the head or through the heart. There were more dead bodies to be added to those already rotting on the sidewalks or at the entrances to houses. "There was an old man shot down in his garden and a woman at the door of their house, a crying woman, who begged me to take care of her husband's body. He had been lying there in front of her for two days." Salam went on to tell of the dead buried one on top of the other for lack of room in the city stadium that had been requisitioned for the purpose. "I saw a car hit by a missile from an Apache helicopter. Inside there were four charred bodies, and on the hood the body of a five-year-old girl. As we approached, our ambulance driver was hit in the shoulder." Farther on a family of twelve, far from the areas where the insurgency was rampant, had been pulverized by a bomb. "I spent the morning putting the bodies back together," the doctor said with a sigh.

As his account went on, his voice cracked with emotion.

Salam had taken photographs of the dead and wounded as evidence. He had kept in his pocket — as a talisman? — a piece of shrapnel picked up next to the body of one of his ambulance workers.

Medicine had not been Dr. Salam's original calling. He would rather have studied design or architecture, but at the insistence of his father, a literature professor, he had studied medicine and become a surgeon. During the invasion, he had spent fifty-five days confined to the hospital of Medical City. The scenes he had just lived through in Fallujah recalled for him his worst moments during the war. But he said that, even then, conditions had been better. Then he had not had to operate on an assembly line in dirty rooms where body parts were piled up, with no disinfectants or analgesics. Right after the war, he and a few colleagues had been called on to manage the Ministry of Health, to distribute the salaries of thousands of doctors in Baghdad, and to conduct investigations of areas contaminated by depleted uranium. He had also organized the program intended to rehouse Arabs driven out of northern Iraq by the Kurds. Then one day, the exiles returned home and took all the ministerial posts, and the young doctor was sent home with a medal.

When I met him, Salam had just received a grant to pursue an advanced degree in London. But he was reluctant to leave home. His parents, who sensed that he was gradually being drawn into the resistance, were urging him to leave, but the corpses of Fallujah obsessed him. A cousin of his had been killed by American soldiers, and there were the inevitable injustices of an occupying army that had grown increasingly brutal as the "resistance" had strengthened. He thought the armed struggle in Iraq needed a political party, a little like Sinn Fein in Northern Ireland. He would have liked to help establish it, to be the Gerry Adams of Iraq.

According to Salam, the siege of Fallujah was unifying the resistance; all the small groups that had until then been acting separately were now joining forces. "The resistance," he said, "has a head and a structure, like a real army." And the old fedayeen of Saddam's army, who represented less than 10 percent of the fighters, were now working hand in hand with the Salafists: a dispiriting assessment confirmed by events in the subsequent months. A short time earlier, despite the disapproval of his rather liberal family, the young doctor himself had joined this strict religious group that was a majority in Fallujah.

Salam assured me that his Salafism was "enlightened," more concerned with combat than with strict obedience to a code he considered too restrictive. "We are educated people, lawyers, doctors, and intellectuals; we shake women's hands and are not obsessed by the length of our dishdashas," the young man with only a trace of a beard explained, perhaps to reassure me. He seemed more fit for the pleasures of his age and for love than for war, "but we have to defend Islam, which they want to destroy." There were also the "foreign fighters," of whom, according to him, there were many in the city. "We brought them in from everywhere, because they are specialists in urban guerrilla warfare," he explained.

I wanted to know how Salam, an "enlightened" anti-American nationalist, reacted to the savagery of the murder of the four American security agents that had preceded the siege and that had so traumatized me.

"It was a barbarous act," he answered. "But you have to understand. Every inhabitant of Fallujah has had a family member executed or arrested by the Americans. We are at war, and those armed men were not civilians. Our fedayeen killed them, and no one came to get the bodies. So some kids who were not very bright and were at loose ends burned their corpses. It was frightful, but it is also frightful to see that for Americans the death of four security agents requires shedding the blood of hundreds of women and children. As though their lives were x times more valuable than ours!"

Looking at his pictures of the wounded children of Fallujah that day, I understood his reasoning. Dr. Salam claimed to hate Saddam, whom he held responsible for the chaos of his country. He was exasperated at hearing the inhabitants of Fallujah described as devotees of the dictator. According to him, Fallujah had become the epicenter of resistance because of the character of its inhabitants. "We are proud and hard, it's true. A little like the Spartans in ancient Greece." Despite the images of dismembered bodies constantly parading before his eyes, despite the tears of his mother who bid him a final farewell every time he left for the accursed city, he was happy to see Iraq finally united. "Today, my entire country, from south to north, is determined to fight those who came to 'liberate' us but ended up killing our women and children." Inspired by his daily proximity to danger and death, he pronounced this somber prophecy: "Americans will win the battle, of course, but by besieging Fallujah they have lost the war."

Even in Baghdad, during the siege of Fallujah, the atmosphere had changed. Streets were deserted. On the roads, you would come across mujahideen in ski masks, with the barrels of rocket launchers sticking out of the windows of their cars. British and South African security agents in the Flowers Hotel across from mine were starting to look more and more like Christmas trees. They walked with their legs bent, covered with straps and Velcro strips holding knives and all sorts of gadgets. You came across strange figures with their revolvers at their belts, bandanas around their heads, and wraparound sunglasses. The arrogance of the private security men in their 4x4's with tinted windows was rampant; frequently they came close to running over pedestrians so they wouldn't have to stop at intersections.

It felt like being in an old western. One day, Muhammad and I had witnessed an incredible scene in front of the Palestine Hotel: American agents in civilian clothes, armed with automatic rifles, had refused to allow themselves to be searched by the Iraqi police at the checkpoint. They had taken up positions with guns pointing against guns, until an American soldier had finally intervened to avoid a bloody showdown.

That day, I was on my way to see Dr. Salam. On the three-lane road running from the neighborhood of my hotel to his house, Muhammad and Stanley and I were dumbfounded at the sight of cars turning around and hightailing it back in the wrong lane. A bit farther on, we found five American tanks blocking the highway. Gunfire and mortar fire erupted near the army barricade, and mujahideen armed with grenade launchers fled in their cars, shaking their fists in our direction. I yelled at Muhammad to turn back. We risked being caught in a crossfire. But he stopped. Muhammad had the defects of his qualities, and all of a sudden he wanted to drop us there in the middle of this madness. The gunfire was coming from his neighborhood, he realized, and he wanted to rush home and make sure his children were safe and sound. In a very quiet voice, knowing it would be useless to shout, I begged him to turn back, and he finally recovered his wits and headed down a side road. When we got to Khazalia, there was an Abrams tank on fire. To destroy this war machine, which deflected shells, the "resisters" had blown up a bridge that had collapsed on top of it. We later learned that the army had to wait until morning to come to the aid of the wounded soldiers inside the wreck. After several hours, we finally reached Salam's home. The whole neighborhood was under strict surveillance: the day before, an American armored vehicle had been hit by the "resistance." During the melee, an old woman living next door to the doctor had been killed.

Three months later in London I saw Dr. Salam again. He had gone there to finish his surgical studies but also to raise funds to establish a hospital for the child amputees of Iraq. An eleven-year-old Iraqi girl, Zeinab, who had lost a leg, was with him. She was cheerful and brave, jumping around laughing on her remaining leg. Her first crutches enchanted her, offering the promise of an almost normal life. Salam still had the same charm and reserve that impressed his interlocutors. He was much more cheerful than he had been in Baghdad. Our reunion was emotional. Everything seemed to be going well for him: A group of reporters and antiwar activists had taken him under their wing. He had met Vanessa Redgrave and had been invited to Stratford to see a performance of *King Lear*. His religious strictness had limits, he explained. He adored opera, especially Rossini's *Barber of Seville*. Someone in London had loaned him a Victorian apartment with a stone terrace opening onto a rose garden. It made me happy to see he had recovered a little of the carefree spirit of his age. If only he could forget his country's ordeal for a moment, study and pursue his medical ambitions. But he was obsessed with the situation in Iraq.

I had come to ask him for letters of recommendation for Fallujah, where I still hoped to go. As soon as the city of his tribe's name was mentioned, his expression changed. He stammered and grew serious. Confronted by my resolve, he offered his blessing, fearfully. Our good-byes were a little too solemn for my taste, as if we were saying good-bye for the last time. Clearly, he disapproved of my seeming obsession with Fallujah, and feared for my life if I went there again.

12

From Nasiriya to Palestine, West Virginia: The Epic Tale of Jessica Lynch
March 2004

THE JESSICA LYNCH STORY had long intrigued me, and as soon as I had a free moment I decided to visit Nasiriya, where the American "heroine's" company had been ambushed, and where the rescue drama had occurred. In a tale worthy of a Hollywood epic, the press and the Pentagon had described her as the first female soldier in enemy hands to have been "liberated" since the Second World War. A raid straight out of an old studio war movie had been organized to attack the Nasiriya hospital where, according to the American military authorities, the young soldier had been held captive, and, it was proclaimed, badly mistreated. My plan was to find and interview the doctor who had cared for her.

Stanley and I were the only guests in the Nasiriya Hotel. I did not feel safe in this small city, which had been heavily bombed and where Shiite parties and their militias proliferated. As I approached the hospital, I saw dirty sheep grazing in the ruins of buildings that had been destroyed during the war. The city had suffered heavy fighting and was looked down on by other Iraqis as the "city of weeds" because of its inhabitants' reputation for stupidity. In the hospital, a large dilapidated building surrounded by empty lots, I was directed to Dr. Harith al-Hussoir, a slender young emergency-room doctor wearing round glasses. He was the one who had treated Jessica Lynch when she recovered consciousness twenty-four hours after arriving at the hospital.

The young doctor seemed like the captain of a ship that was adrift. He was everywhere at once, receiving the wounded, checking X-rays, operating. What is more, he had a sense of humor. Experienced beyond his years, he had become cynical but not disillusioned under Saddam's dictatorship, and then through the war and the occupation. He had an acute sense of the absurdity of the sequence of events through which he had just lived. He broke out in happy laughter, which he unsuccessfully tried to stifle, when he told me the story of his war. His laughter was infectious, and we laughed together about the Ubuesque "war" he described in the filthy hospital room in Nasiriya.

The doctor recalled how surprised he had been when the first casualties arrived in Nasiriya. Iraqi television had not even mentioned the advance of American troops. He had driven an ambulance thirty miles east of the city, where Iraqi police officers told him there were some wounded Americans, and a soldier from Mosul whose legs had been blown off by an explosion. Harith had returned to the hospital: as a civilian doctor, he was not responsible for wounded soldiers. But he reported what he had heard to the director of the hospital, who, to Harith's astonishment, burst into tears. He begged Harith to keep quiet: if he repeated in the presence of an official of the Baath Party the fact that Americans were there, all the staff of the hospital risked prison or even death for treason, on the grounds of playing into the hands of the enemy by confirming their propaganda. The director of the hospital even went so far as to threaten the doctor with punishment "after the war" if he spilled the beans.

"Americans were in the city, but if you had the misfortune to say so to the men who were supposed to defend us, you were subject to the death penalty," the doctor now said, bemused. The Iraqi army had soon moved into the hospital and lived there with the doctors and their families. After March 20, new supplies stopped arriving. "Day and night we took in casualties; we had nearly three hundred civilians in serious condition."

Four days after the bombing of Nasiriya began, the doctor remembered seeing Jessica Lynch being brought in. One day the military hierarchy had informed the doctors that they were about to receive a very important patient. Harith thought they were talking about Saddam's cousin "Chemical Ali." After being ordered to clear the emergency room, he saw two young women being brought in on stretchers. One, Lori Piestewa, was already dead. The other had a head wound and had lost a lot of blood. The doctor gave her a transfusion of two liters of blood, "blood from the hospital's medical personnel," he pointed out. Twenty-four hours later, Jessica Lynch came to. "The first words she said were, 'I'm afraid.' I asked her what she was afraid of, and she said: 'Saddam.'"

On the X-ray, the doctor saw she had a cranial trauma and arm and leg fractures caused by her truck accident, but no bullet wounds. The young soldier was depressed and constantly in tears. "I took care of her like a baby. I arranged her pillows so she could see the city from her bed. I brought her crackers and orange juice and assured her that she would be evacuated soon."

When he thought she was able to travel, he tried to organize her transfer by ambulance to an American checkpoint. It was no use — greeted by gunfire, the ambulance had to turn back. The rest of the story is well known: a nighttime raid that shook the hospital, doors broken down, and the evacuation of the soldier.

When I met him, Harith still didn't understand. "They knew she was on the second floor but didn't know that the Iraqi soldiers had left the hospital several days earlier?" On the day of the raid, some doctors were confined for four hours. The assistant director of the hospital was released by the soldiers only seven days later.

On April 1, President Bush announced to the American people the liberation of a female soldier of the 507th Company who had been held prisoner since March 23. A week later, the Pentagon gave the press a video taken during the rescue. In this Hollywood war movie, filmed in night vision, you see a whole army of Special Forces officers assaulting the hospital where Jessica was "held captive." Meanwhile, on April 3, a front-page article in the *Washington Post* had launched the "epic tale" of Jessica's rescue. The article quoted an official source, who asserted: "She fought to the death. She didn't want to be taken alive." The legend of Jessica had been born. In one paraphrase or another, the entire world press asserted that Jessica had fought fiercely, that she had emptied the magazine of her M-16 at the enemy, and that, wounded by several bullets and stabbed, she had finally been taken to a hospital, the headquarters of the enemy forces, where she had been beaten, mistreated, and perhaps raped.

It should be recalled that at that point in the war, the euphoria of the first days of the offensive was far behind. Americans had not been welcomed as "liberators" as expected, to almost universal surprise. On television we were shown distressing pictures of the terrified face of Shoshana Johnson, another soldier taken prisoner by the Iraqis. It is clear that, two weeks after the beginning of the war in Iraq, the violent liberation of Jessica Lynch by the Special Forces provided patriotic balm for the army's wounded pride.

The soldier's story calmed the nation's anxiety. Oliver North, who had turned into an embedded reporter for Fox News during the war, grew fiery in the *Washington Times:* "We hope that the bravery [of Jessica's rescuers] will give the lie to the stories that skeptical scribes have recently scribbled in the press. The war is a successful military campaign, planned by talented officers and executed by the best fighters in the world."

But on May 15 a report entitled "The Truth about Jessica" in the British daily the *Guardian* tarnished if not destroyed the legend: an investigation by reporter John Kampfner in Nasiriya, broadcast on the BBC on May 18, presented Dr. Harith's version. On June 17 the *Washington Post*, returning to what had become the "Lynch affair," quoted a colonel who blamed the press for having embellished the "Jessica fable."

When he spoke to me, Dr. Harith was surprised not to have received a word of thanks for having taken such good care of the

American heroine. The only person to receive a reward and American citizenship was the Iraqi lawyer who alerted the marines to where she was. Dr. Harith explained to me that the lawyer's only role was to have caught sight of the American during a visit to the hospital. He still had enough of a sense of humor to see the irony of the situation. "Don't you find it comic to think that that man, a former member of Saddam's secret services, is wanted by the inhabitants of Nasiriya for the harassment to which he subjected them, and now he's presented as a saint in the United States?"

The doctor then grew serious. The "Lynch affair" was the least of his concerns. He started to give me a tour of the hospital, but immediately left me to take care of an emergency. The dilapidated state of the hospital gave me chills. Even in the most distant corners of Afghanistan I had never seen anything like it. Rubbish was burning outside the entrance. The filthy emergency room was crowded. Tension was mounting, and a doctor signaled to me that I should leave immediately. Every day doctors were attacked by patients frustrated by the waiting and the lack of medicine. Many of them were armed, and there was no security service at the hospital. If anyone decided to go after me, the doctors would be incapable of defending me. And the sharp, revolting odor of blood and urine mixed with the smell of corpses forced visitors and patients to cover their faces with damp cloths. On the fourth floor we visited the amputees. The ward was full of flies and, again, the odor was stifling. In the corridor, about fifteen women were squatting in the filth, wrapped in their *abayas*. When Stanley arrived, they huddled together like a rugby team in a scrum, so that all that could be seen was a patchwork of black cloth. Here, everything was wanting. The young doctor stated unequivocally that the situation of the hospital had deteriorated terribly since the fall of Saddam. "The Italians brought us a small quantity of medicine. But we sometimes see two thousand patients a day in this hospital. You might as well try to feed a family of fifty with a sandwich."

The destitution and filth removed the scene far from the

sanitized vision of a Hollywood war. In the Nasiriya museum, Stanley had broken down when he saw the broken bottles and remains of meals soiling the Sumerian antiquities. For me, this hospital was where I wanted to scream, listening to the story in which the wicked were honored and the heroes hunted down, while the "nice guys" managed without anything, engulfed in odors of piss and death.

Nine months earlier, in July 2003, I had gone to Jessica Lynch's hometown. I wanted to see how the Fourth of July was cele-brated in the birthplace of the "American Joan of Arc." I wanted to witness the celebration of the patriotic holiday in the most pa-triotic county in the United States, and I was not disappointed. Of course, in this fertile rural countryside, the residents' pride was clearly displayed on all the billboards on the way into town. Palestine, Wirt County, West Virginia, "birthplace of former prisoner of war Jessica Lynch."

I didn't have to worry about eliciting any acrimony by iden-tifying my nationality. No one there knew France's position on the war. In front of the houses, between signs asserting ABOR-TION IS A CRIME and GOD IS IN CONTROL, posters thanked the Lord for having saved "Jessie" and expressed support for the sol-diers still in Iraq and Afghanistan. The ubiquitous religiosity, the atmosphere of the end of the world and the end of the war, made me feel uncomfortable. But at a moment when the entire coun-try was wrapped in the flag, in the story of the Pentagon's hero-ine, I found that this celebration was oddly quiet. There had been no fireworks in Elizabeth, the county seat, no speeches, just a nice little parade and a modest picnic on the lawn outside the barracks. "We don't know when Jessie's coming back. Even her parents have disappeared," I was told by Paula, a teacher's assis-tant wearing a dress made from an American flag, to explain the lack of excitement.

I asked the group gathered around the orchestra if any of them thought that the soldier's adventure had been slightly em-bellished by the Pentagon's communications experts and by the press. At that, everyone sitting near Paula on the lawn had lowered his head. For the inhabitants of Elizabeth, doubting the epic tale of the young heroine seemed as obscene as doubting the love of one's country.

And yet, there were some who asked questions. What had really happened to Jessie? They both pitied and envied the poor local girl who had become famous and thus rich. Since the news of her "rescue," Jessie, the little soldier who had joined the army to finance her education and become a teacher, had been overcome by events. The hawks in the Pentagon had made her the muse of their war, and for the pacifists she was the personification of the most shameful propaganda. Even in her hometown, "Jessicagate" had divided neighbors. For even in this patriotic heartland, some people quietly agreed with the very shocking position of their senator, Robert Byrd. His March 19 speech, which began with the words "Today, I cried for my country," had been taken up by pacifists around the world.

"You know, many of our children have gone or will go to Afghanistan, Iraq, or maybe Africa. It's the only way we have to give them a decent life. So of course we're tired of worrying about them," one resident explained, as though to excuse himself for supporting the iconoclastic senator.

Going to war in order not to die of hunger. One-fifth of the inhabitants of Wirt County were living below the poverty line. In Palestine, the unemployment rate was close to 15 percent. In the streets of Jessica Lynch's hometown, the everyday poverty of the people left behind by the American dream was blindingly obvious. I saw trailers carting water in buckets, stores with broken windows, and many "For Sale" signs. The only store in town still open had a name that didn't encourage consumption: "What You No Longer Want." In Palestine, USA, I had the impression that the town itself had shut up shop.

Next to the little town swimming pool, I met Tina, a logger's wife who was washing cars. She and a few friends were trying to raise money for one of her husband's coworkers who had been hit by a falling tree. Neighbors helping each other was the only way to survive. Not long before, Tina had been washing cars so David Bell's mother could go see her son in the hospital. The young soldier had just had a cheek shot off in Afghanistan. "The Pentagon people did nothing for him, but he was a hero too, wasn't he? Jessica's relatives all have new cars." The young woman sighed as she wiped a windshield. "Why the favoritism?" she asked, and she answered her own question in a way that pretty well summed up the whole Lynch affair: "Because she's a pretty girl and her story made us feel good at a time when the country wasn't doing so well over there in Iraq."

13

The Iraqi Auxiliaries
July 2004

THIS WAS THE SEVENTH TIME I'd been to Iraq. As always, I felt a combination of excitement and terror, as though I were about to jump from a plane without knowing whether my parachute would open. Would I succeed in accomplishing the task I had set myself? Was it pure recklessness that subjected my family to yet another test? Some of my friends had decided that this risk taking reflected my need to prove, by putting my life in danger, that it was worth living. My behavior resembled a medieval ordeal by fire, and provided confirmation that I had been favored at least by luck. A few days before leaving, all these questions returned to torment me and weaken my resolve. But I knew they would disappear once I was on the plane. This psychological blessing always surprised me — your heart hardens once you've reached the point of no return, and you think only of doing what you've set out to do despite all obstacles. And this kind of war reporting is nothing but a series of obstacle courses. Sometimes my own hardness frightened me; I felt alienated from myself. But this was also one of the reasons why I loved war reporting — there is no room for doubt, you are nothing but a machine moving toward a single goal.

Flying from Amman to Baghdad, I thought in terror of the dives the plane would have to make when landing to avoid missiles. I also remembered the oppressive heat that awaited me. It was the middle of July, and to the usual difficulties would be added the unbearable temperature that made you move in slow motion like someone imprisoned in a sauna. I was the only woman on the plane. Fifty husky South African mercenaries spent the journey in silence. Nor did the few Iraqi businessmen, dozing in their seats, exchange a word. Like everyone else, I tried to relax.

In the center of Baghdad the first thing I noticed, in this period following the transfer of power, was the low profile of the coalition forces' tanks. Even in front of the fortress of the Palestine Hotel, the dozen Humvees that had replaced the two tanks stationed on the square gave an impression of lightness. In the oppressive heat of the afternoon, the streets were deserted. As I had on every previous return, I wanted to believe that things were improving. It was almost peace, barely troubled by police patrols, Iraqi army checkpoints, and the two Australian tanks encountered on the road from the airport. Even the private guards protecting foreigners seemed to be carrying their weapons more discreetly. The cowboys had put away their paraphernalia, and everyone was following the coalition's instructions to be low-key. Some men had parked a car on the Jadriya Bridge, which had been strictly prohibited under Saddam. They were looking at the river and drinking alcohol, giving me a picture of freedom. But, as always, this was an illusion. The coalition forces had stepped up patrols in trouble spots like Khazalia and Haifa Street, where there were almost daily raids. And tanks coming from nowhere, from bases concealed from the inhabitants' view, soon created a feeling of unease. The masters of the city were still there, just invisible — hidden away, like Saddam in his palaces, and like the intangible sense of danger.

Foreigners, afraid of being kidnapped, had deserted the restaurants. And Iraqis cast dark looks at the few who did venture into them, because by doing so they endangered everyone. But there was no choice. I knew that after a few days I, too, would be ready to take any risk to avoid the hotel's stale hummus, overcooked spaghetti, and white Formica tables. The troop of translators and drivers working for foreign diplomats and reporters was under increasing threat. The translator I had stumbled on, afraid of stray bullets, asked me to walk ten paces in front of him in the street. In al-Mansur we saw a burned-out video game store, and Muhammad told me that its owner had lost a leg in the explosion. A few days later, we learned that the poor man had lost the other leg in an attack on the hospital where he had been taken.

In the Hotel al-Hamra, I saw the same faces I had seen since the beginning of the Iraq war. There was Samir, the Christian pianist, with his black ponytail and his face ravaged by alcohol, who told me every time I came that I would never see him again, because he'd gotten his visa for the United States, where his career as a concert pianist would take off. He seemed more depressed this time. Sipping his whiskey at the side of the pool, he told me, again, the story of his life, as though I had forgotten it. How he had bayoneted an Iranian during the war, despite his loathing of violence; how he'd been a gigolo in Italy before returning to his country. And as he had always done before, he urged me to go back home. There was Rita, whom I'd first met during the war in the north, doing laps in the pool around eleven at night, the only time when it was bearable to be outside. I saw a new face by the side of the pool, Sharleen, a blond photographer from Oregon in her forties, who had come to do a feature on American soldiers. She was crying, but the hot wind instantly dried her tears. She told me that the young woman who had been translating for her had been assassinated. She seemed lost, alone, and scared to death.

The next day I went to Camp Victory, the big U.S. base near the airport, for a report on the training of the new Iraqi army by the coalition forces. When I got there, Captain Smith told me that all routine patrols had been suspended. A major raid was about to be launched on the town that, second only to Fallujah, was the most dangerous spot in Iraq. In Abu Ghraib, the town where the notorious prison was located, the effect produced by the photographs of the abuse inflicted by American soldiers had been even more devastating than elsewhere. In April the coalition had killed more than five hundred Sunni and Shiite insurgents who had joined forces in the town. Two hundred Iraqi soldiers in the "new army" and eighty American soldiers were to participate in the upcoming raid. The plan was to arrest insurgents who had been involved in several mortar attacks on the American camp near Abu Ghraib.

Captain Smith asked me if I wanted to go with them. I had already done that several times, and had told myself that I would never again be a living target in a raid that was like playing Russian roulette. All such raids were pretty much alike: a deadly combination of tedium and extreme danger. But this, I was told, would be different, a combined raid of Iraqi and American soldiers. So I accepted.

Smith, the American instructor, with blond hair, pale blue eyes, and clipped military speech, loved his job. He told me he had decided to join the army after a suicide attempt at the age of fifteen. "I asked God to show me the way. He told me to join the infantry." God again, always God. Smith was in the army and in Iraq in the name of God, like so many other soldiers I had met who had explained that they were following the Lord's mysterious plan in waging this war. To train his men, some of whom were barely eighteen, Smith used a close-combat video game called Computer Gate. "That way, their first fight takes place on a computer. Nothing bears a closer resemblance to combat than a video game," he told me. When I had first played the game and shot a machine gun from a tank, I had the same thought. Dr. Salam had sent me some film taken from an American plane flying over Fallujah, in which you could see people being targeted and then bombed, with the pilot icily talking about "taking them out." For Salam, these were his cousins being eliminated like ants when sprayed; for the soldiers they were distant and almost virtual targets.

Smith claimed that he respected his 240 Iraqi soldiers. They had "conducted themselves well" every time they had been shot at. But he had no illusions about their motives. "They're here for the pay" — $150 per month for the lower ranks — "exactly like the Americans. Very few of us are here to defend their country," he acknowledged.

The most difficult thing for him was to separate the wheat from the chaff. "Some of them are informers in the pay of insurgents. You know, there aren't very many innocent people in this country." Besides, in his opinion, the last group of soldiers that had joined were giving information to the local sheikhs. Colonel Mohammed, the Iraqi in command of the 303rd Battalion, didn't want to sign them up for that reason, "but the American command decided otherwise to please some tribal leaders," he explained. Captain Smith pointed out a husky, sinister-looking recent recruit who answered to the name of Abu Brahim. "Iraqis have intelligent hoodlums. Unfortunately, they're the ones fighting against us." According to him, the American command made them take on this sergeant because he was the protégé of the sheikh of an influential tribe. But everyone in the camp was suspicious of him, and they were convinced he was providing intelligence to the "terrorists." I looked in fascination at the face of this man, covered with scars. His men said that he was a former member of Saddam's special forces. "To toughen us up, they had us kill animals and eat them raw," one of his former companions boasted. But Abu Brahim refused to talk to me about that period in his life. Because he was considered a "collaborator" of the Americans, his house had been hit by mortars five times. The last time, his mother had been wounded and a nephew killed. Like his men, he complained about living conditions, and about his pay, which was not enough to justify the risks he ran. "Under Saddam we got a plot of land and a sum of money. We're not as well paid now as the police." He also complained about the obsolete weapons and the presence of women in the unit, a novelty introduced by the Americans that exasperated him. "We're heroes. Why do we need women? They only complicate the work." Obviously this NCO in command of a platoon was nostalgic for the Saddam years. "Then, when we made complaints to our general, he settled things in a few days," he explained. There was also the nagging question of the transfer of power, and the constant humiliation of being commanded by Americans, even here where relations between the men were better than elsewhere.

I found Iraqi soldiers puzzling. Before long they began asking me, a foreign journalist, to record their complaints, about their equipment, their pay, and their life as pariahs. Some of them didn't even bother concealing their nostalgia for Saddam's time. If they were to be believed, the only difference for them since the fall of the dictator was that they could wear sunglasses during operations. So they went overboard with sunglasses — they squeezed their imitation Ray-Bans, Calvin Kleins, and Oakleys between masks and bandanas, making them look like actors playing "war in Iraq."

But what most distressed them was their sexual misery. "Even the gypsies in the camps around here won't come near us because we're traitors," one of them told me. "Can you ask the captain to let us have sexual relations with the female soldiers?" He looked disappointed when I explained that I wasn't sure I could persuade the captain to grant this request.

Suddenly it was time to get ready. I loved this feverish activity: men who had been whining a moment earlier were now gearing up to face danger without a word. Despite their inadequate equipment, the men seemed happy to go into battle. They carefully concealed their faces so that no one would be able to recognize them. Ali, one of the soldiers, asked to exchange bandanas with me for luck.

Iraqi soldiers looked enviously at my bulletproof vest with its metal plate. One of them politely offered me a Kalashnikov: he wasn't sure he could defend me in case of an attack. This was touching, but his concern did little to reassure me. The Americans piled into their armored vehicles. Only Captain Smith, the instructor of the Iraqi soldiers, like us and "his men," got into a Datsun pickup truck with its windows open, at the mercy of a grenade. There I was, back in the thick of things!

On board the unprotected vehicle, I knew I was a living target. I thought about Muhammad, who had gone off on his own, and hoped that we would meet up in one piece at the end of the day. And then I tuned in to the music coming from the truck's radio and felt my adrenaline rising. I wanted to sing along with the soldiers.

Eight "objectives" had been identified in one of the neighborhoods of Abu Ghraib — "mortar launchers," explained an Iraqi soldier, who had his radio blasting to distract him from his fear. When we got to the spot, the American Humvees and tanks already had their guns trained on the houses, and helicopters were flying over the area. Captain Smith lectured the Iraqi officers who were supposed to be supervising the operation. One of them was directing traffic instead of directing his men. One platoon had lingered in a house and lost the rest of the troop. The whole thing was a little bizarre, but there was no major clash. The raid was well conducted. Men were caught in the shower; mothers sobbed when their sons were arrested, and begged me to help them because I was a woman, because I looked different, and because I stroked the children's heads as though to dissociate myself from the soldiers I was with.

Whether conducted by Iraqis or Americans, all raids were alike, and they all provoked the same feeling of discomfort. I wanted to beg people's pardon for being there, distance myself from the breaking down of doors, the violence of armed men searching all the corners of the houses they attacked in the stifling heat of the siesta of a Friday after prayers — the best time to act, according to American soldiers. On this day, eight men were arrested. One of them was thrown into our truck. An Iraqi soldier signaled that I should hand over my scarf to blindfold him. I complied. The gesture was not innocent; it pushed me over to the soldiers' side, and my feeling of discomfort increased.

Back in camp, Captain Smith declared his satisfaction: the operation had lasted less than an hour. But over at Camp Bravo, home of the 303rd Battalion, twenty-five angry Iraqi soldiers were assembled in front of the gates, an entire platoon in revolt.

These soldiers, humiliated men who wanted reparation, all wanted to talk to me. One of them, Hassan, described the corruption undermining the unit. He claimed that one of the sergeants and seven other Iraqi soldiers were taking commissions on contracts, and they were selling on the black market the weapons they seized. "When we denounced these practices, the Americans confined us to quarters. They aimed their guns at us and insulted us. One of them spit at me. And I discovered three car bombs last month. One of the American soldiers, Captain Mike, was furious; he asked his compatriots why they were humiliating us like that and he threatened to leave. So they arrested him, too."

Far from being embarrassed by these revelations, the sentries at Camp Bravo were sympathetic. "The Americans control everything. As far as we're concerned, there's no transfer of power, just a transfer of risk. We're nothing but their human shields. Two days ago, I went on patrol with them. They were in armored vehicles, and we were in pickup trucks. And, of course, our men were killed when the bomb went off," one of them told me.

In Camp Bravo, I also met Sheikh al-Dulaimi. With his majestic traditional robes and his blue eyes, he looked like a movie star. As he did every week, the president of the National League of Sheikhs had come to negotiate with the Americans for the release of prisoners from Abu Ghraib. Since the scandal of the photographs of torture in the prison that once symbolized the cruelty of Saddam's regime, inmates had been released by the busload. Tribal leaders guaranteed their good behavior in writing, and that was all it took. Sometimes arrangements were made even before men guilty of acts of resistance were arrested. Sheikh al-Dulaimi was one of the principal architects of this new American pragmatism. Since the transfer of power, he had helped some of Saddam's former intelligence agents find work. Every day, hundreds of petitioners came to his offices looking for his support to rejoin the administration or the army. "Reinstating former members of the Baath Party is the only way Americans can hope to restore peace in Iraq," said the sheikh. Still, one might wonder what good it had been to dismantle the regime only to gradually reinstate its most brutal elements.

For his part, Captain Smith could not stomach the inclusion in the ranks of the new army of former officials of Saddam's regime who, a few months earlier, had been considered the enemy. "To tell you the truth," he commented wryly, "I would never have imagined that one day it would be my duty to train war criminals."

14

Dispatches
June 2005

Back to Iraq. This time I had told only my closest friends and my three editors that I was going. I had no desire to face the distressed looks of my friends and colleagues or to listen to their protests — which, since some French reporters had been taken hostage in Iraq, had become openly aggressive. The French government had paid millions of dollars to free two of my colleagues, and there was talk of a similar sum for the ransom of Florence Aubenas, correspondent for *La Libération*, who had been held hostage for five months and would be freed a few days after my arrival in June. "Why are you doing this, and what good does it do, finally, to take so many risks? Are you sure you'll be able to do your job?" Reporters who wanted to go to Iraq were treated as irresponsible people who risked depleting the country's finances, not to mention complicating its foreign policy.

Since beginning my Iraq adventure, I had felt both charged with a mission and caught in a deadly trap. Nearly sixty reporters had already been killed in Iraq, and there were few candidates to replace them. My mother was in New York, protected by distance from her friends' expressions of distress. I sympathized with her anxiety: I recognized that I wouldn't want to have a daughter doing my job. My editors, who at first tried to dissuade me from going, were reassured because I would be embedded with the 42nd Infantry Division. I had not explained in detail that, although I would not be in danger of being kidnapped, going on patrol with living targets was just as risky.

I had decided to go in spite of the danger, perhaps because being a war correspondent was all I knew, and also because it was a sovereign remedy against the anguish of being alive. When you concentrate on staying alive for the next hour, oddly enough you forget that you are eventually going to die in any event. When I was there, I stopped consuming myself with worry about my daughter, my friends, my family. War reporting took my all; it was better than Prozac.

I persuaded Stanley Greene to come with me again. I admired him for having accepted: at the age of fifty-six, he hadn't hesitated to leave the trailer he lived in in Mexico to slog through Iraq with the soldiers. Would he be able to carry his gear, crawl through the mud of the palm groves? He turned out to be much more resilient than I. He went on all the patrols; once he came back from a patrol through the swamps near Baquba not having changed his clothes for two days — they were his war trophy. He arrived in Kuwait City wearing his leather jacket and rings on every finger, gifts warmly given by rebels around the world. We made our final purchases in the giant malls of this consumers' paradise: a flashlight with a red beam because white light was against the rules on military bases, ear plugs for riding in helicopters, combat goggles for Humvee patrols, high-tech underwear to put on under bulletproof vests.

Because we had come against the advice of everyone, we were more anxious than usual. Even Yan, who had always supported my ventures to Iraq, seemed worried this time. The frenzy of shopping hadn't completely calmed us down, and I asked Stanley to stop talking about his girlfriend, who had told him she would see him in heaven if anything happened to him.

When we left the next day, the hotel concierge said goodbye with a look of distress. An employee of KBR, who arranged military flights to Baghdad and had seen all the reporters and contractors killed in Iraq come through his office, warned us to be especially careful. He talked to us again about the four contractors whose charred bodies we had seen in the streets of Fallujah.

This was the first time we had put faces and names on the dead men. In a few hours, a Hercules C-130 would take us to Iraq.

Because this was the first time for many of the soldiers flying with us, we soon blended into the crowd. We had the same fears, all of us riveted by terror. It was ideal for my reporting, because I felt what the soldiers felt. I would be treated as they were, at least until we got to Baghdad. But when the plane doors closed, it felt like a nightmare. I wanted to shout that this was a case of mistaken identity, like the character in *Hair* sent to Vietnam in his friend's place. I took out my ear plugs to listen to the pilot shouting his instructions above the engine noise: "If you're going to Baghdad, it's not your lucky day, guys. There's a nasty sandstorm. It'll take us the whole day and it won't be fun. Put on your seat belts or you'll get thrown around. No vomiting in the oxygen bags. The last time, I had to clean twenty of them, and they cost four hundred bucks apiece."

Stanley and I were crowded on the benches of the Hercules with our gear and sixty soldiers, heading for Basra, Kirkuk, and finally Baghdad. Once the huge cargo door was closed, I felt as though I were trapped inside an oven. I took shallow breaths of the humid air, hoping I would be able to make it. We had been advised to sit on our bulletproof vests to protect ourselves from stray bullets from below. I squeezed in among helmets, M-16s, my neighbors' legs, and the large backpacks hanging from hooks, soldiers' equipment for a one-year tour of duty. Some of them were coming back for the second or third time, having reenlisted or back from leave. And then there were the new ones, immediately recognizable. They perspired more than the others, and looked around for an air vent or a smile from their sergeant.

On my left, soldier B, who worked in a Ford plant in Kentucky, helped me buckle my shoulder belt. The heat had given him a nosebleed, he'd grown pale, and he seemed about to be sick. His bulletproof vest had fallen at his feet. Seeing him in that condition worried me: if he couldn't hold up, what chance did I have? Sitting across from him, his sergeant, Sergeant Britton, a large man with a plug of chewing tobacco in his cheek, comforted him with a loud laugh: "Hey soldier, you want to lose your ass?"

"No, sergeant, I love my ass, but this damn vest is killing me; I'm thirsty, I'm on fire."

"Don't worry, I'll take care of you in Baghdad."

"He'll keep me out of trouble. It'll be all right," B, calmer now, said to me with a wan smile.

As for Britton, with his shaved head, the tobacco he chewed continuously as though it were khat, his loud laughter at every jolt of the Hercules that gave us the feeling we were about to crash, by the end of the trip I adored him. "I hope we'll meet again in more pleasant circumstances," he said when we arrived in Baghdad. "Try to stay alive, OK?"

"Be safe" was the constant refrain of soldiers in Iraq. Every meeting was punctuated with "Be safe," "Don't take too many risks," "I hope I'll see you safe and sound." Signs of affection or politeness, I had heard these formulas spoken in every tone of voice. But they were empty words, as bizarre as being told to stay dry in the middle of a downpour. "Be safe out there," they said. They said "out there," but I knew they meant in this quagmire.

Hell for the soldiers in Baghdad started with waiting. Soldiers not stationed in the capital had to find a plane or helicopter to take them to their base. Sometimes they would have to camp on the airport runway for three days in the hot yellow dust of a sandstorm, waiting for a possible flight. And then they had to know where they were going. We were trying to get to Tikrit, Saddam's birthplace, his lair where he had built a network of palaces. Hard as it was to believe, no one had heard of it. "Tikrit? Can you spell that? Is it the same thing as Kirkuk? Where is it, in what FOB?"

We soon got used to the geography of this new world, not really American, certainly not Iraqi: the map of bases covering occupied Iraq. Baghdad, Basra, and Kirkuk had been replaced by FOB (Forward Operations Base) Viper, Pale Horse, and Warrior. I had gone through the looking glass. Since road convoys had become much too risky, we made short hops with soldiers in

Black Hawks between these little pieces of America. The camp in Baghdad was so large that bus lines connected its various sections. Radio Freedom broadcast the news of this strange world into which I had been plunged. After a few days on the base shopping, doing laundry, and going to the movies, you could almost forget that there was a war on the other side of the barriers surrounding the camp. Even the currency was special. When the Pakistanis or Filipinos running the stores didn't have change for our dollars, they gave us little cardboard tokens with pictures of Humvees or soldiers. As for Tikrit, I learned that its name matched its reputation: FOB Danger.

To get there, I stood on the runway in single file with the soldiers, wearing a helmet and like them carrying a heavy backpack, ninja turtles who terrified the vulnerable Iraqis in their simple white robes. It had taken me a solid minute after I put on my pack to recover my balance. Stanley too was struggling not to fall over backward. I tried to resist the hot blasts of sand from helicopters taking off and landing. "I'm going to die from the heat in this goddamn vest!" I muttered. Stanley flinched and ordered me not to use such language. Like the soldiers, he was getting superstitious, looking for signs: "If I take fifteen more steps before I get in the copter, then everything will be all right." But despite the danger threatening us, anticipating the flight made us feel almost giddy. "Flying in a Black Hawk is something I love and hate at the same time," a colonel explained. "For all my men, it's a reward. A reward they sometimes pay a heavy price for when there's an attack."

It was summer, and we flew with all doors open, our feet hanging in space and the wind whistling through our helmets. It was unreal, and I had to keep reminding myself that I was actually there, living through this bizarre adventure. A few days earlier, a single machine gun bullet in an engine had turned a helicopter into a crumpled piece of charred metal, with no survivors.

Despite this story, which everyone had been talking about, I stopped calculating our chances of dying suddenly, burned up in a furnace, and forced myself to take pleasure in our flight. Pilots

flew at barely a hundred yards above ground in order not to give
the enemy the opportunity to prepare an attack too far in advance. From takeoff, the noise of the rotors and the distance gave
me the impression that I was in a war movie rather than the war
itself. Soldiers were taking pictures. Even the Darth Vader in
front of me in his black helmet, pointing his machine gun toward
the ground, seemed to appreciate the landscape. I recognized the
streets of Baghdad and the Palestine Hotel, and then the fields of
sunflowers, the luxuriant foliage of the palm groves of Baquba,
and finally the string of Saddam's palaces in Tikrit. Children
were playing in the emerald waters of the meandering river. According to Vietnam veterans now serving in Iraq, this spot on the
Tigris recalled the Mekong Delta. For the first time I saw that
Iraq was a beautiful country.

My editors had asked me to be embedded with American
soldiers, to try to understand their motives, to make them talk. I
knew that it would be easy to live in harmony with the soldiers.
My reporting in Iraq had taught me time and again that everything was a matter of viewpoint. Conditioned by fear and the
strong bonds created by danger, one ended up seeing the world
like the people one was with. This recognition was troubling. If
you can share all the points of view of the various sides, then the
temptation is to fall into absolute relativism. Is there no truth? Is
no cause just? Does might make right?

The sense of family, solidarity across generations, hospitality erected into a philosophy and an art of living, had more than
once given me a glimpse of the superiority of some Eastern ways
of life over Western customs. The one thing I had trouble accepting among both Iraqis and Americans was the feeling on
both sides that in this war they were carrying out the will of God.
I was resistant to what I saw as an ideology, not only because reference to the Crusades and the Inquisition evoked negative images, but because it precluded any discussion.

When I got to Tikrit, I was taken to Saddam's principal
palace, overlooking a hill, now the headquarters of the 42nd Infantry Division. My memories of Tikrit during the war overlaid

what I saw now. During the war, the palace had been swarming with soldiers dumbfounded at the opulence and bad taste of Saddam's living quarters. A strange atmosphere now prevailed in the nearly deserted marble and concrete corridors. Three days earlier, a suicide bomber had blown himself up at the entrance to the base. And the day before our arrival, two officers, Captain Phillip Esposito and First Lieutenant Louis Allen, had been killed in their room at ten at night by what appeared to have been a mortar shell.

A mysterious silence I couldn't explain surrounded this tragic event, banal as it was in the Iraqi context. I later learned that the soldiers could not answer my questions because an investigation was under way. I would pass soldiers whispering in the corridors of the palace like characters in an Agatha Christie novel. At first I thought I was projecting my own unease. In any case, it was bizarre to be in Iraq without really being there, unable to see my friends, and to see the country only through the windshield of a Humvee. I no longer knew where I was, plunged into a virtual world in which the actors had been changed as if by magic. I had known Tikrit in Saddam's time, Tikrit with the Iraqis during and after the war, and now I was in the Tikrit of the Americans.

But the feeling of being in Kafka's castle didn't come from my unease alone. The attack that had killed the two officers the day before was the first case of fragging in Iraq. Had the murderer, a soldier named Martinez with money problems, been refused leave or an advance by his commander? This was a military secret, and I would be told nothing.

When he greeted me in the palace, Captain Giordano was still in a state of shock: Esposito had died in his arms. He was profoundly upset and fed up with this place where the enemy was everywhere and at the same time invisible. "I hate war," he confessed.

When I expressed surprise that there were no Iraqis on the bases where, the last time I had been here, they did odd jobs for the soldiers, he explained that since a suicide bomber had killed twenty-two people, including fourteen American soldiers, and wounded sixty-nine in the dining facility in Mosul, the Iraqis had been kept away from American bases. Everyone was afraid of spies.

At FOB Danger, soldiers gulped down their meals in less than five minutes to reduce the risks. But that evening Colonel Boyd, a reserve officer and military historian who had written a dissertation on the neutrality of Kentucky during the American Civil War, with whom I was having dinner, was disposed to take his time. He talked endlessly about the Civil War and his childhood. He had decided — out of sheer superstition — not to go to bed before ten-thirty, the time of his comrades' death the night before. In the moonlight, we walked down the little path leading from the dining hall to the palace. The colonel loaded his revolver and complained about the rule keeping officers of his rank from having an M-16 on the base. "I don't like this path. We're a target. Anyway, I could keep them from kidnapping us," he said protectively, unholstering his weapon. Distraught, he told me he'd seen it all: "I've seen people who have a greater will to fight because of their dead, and people who despair because of their dead." He had volunteered to come because one of his beloved students, named Jeff, had been killed in Baghdad. "Jeff's head was blown off by a shell. And yet, when he left home I wasn't worried about him. Six months before, his brother had committed suicide, hanged himself. To make matters worse, his mother had found him. I thought, no, not twice in the same family. Both of them have been laid to rest in a cemetery in Kentucky. Near Daniel Boone."

The first Iraqi I finally met on a Tikrit base was a wounded soldier in the base hospital, who had stepped on a mine. His body was surrounded by drains, pouches, and tubes, and the respirator sounded like a bellows. With a desperate cough, he tried to clear his throat. He had been there for a month. As I continued through the hospital, I stopped to visit two American soldiers with burns and contusions, whose Humvee had been hit by an explosive device, and who had just been wheeled into a small adjoining room. The next day, doctors told me they were going to operate on an American soldier who had been hit at the base of the penis, narrowly escaping the wound that is every soldier's nightmare.

Stanley had been able to photograph the severely wounded Iraqi soldier from every angle, but he couldn't get near the Americans. He had been instructed not to document our visit in the hospital, to protect the families and not weaken troop morale. Of course I understood, but the double standard made me uneasy, since the great majority of the wounded and dead were now Iraqi soldiers. It was as though the lives of these auxiliaries were not as valuable as those of American soldiers. The Iraqi's wounds were very severe, but he would not be evacuated to Germany because he was Iraqi. I wondered at what point this great melting pot of an army had begun to turn in on itself and adopt racist practices reminiscent of the attitude of the French army in Algeria back in the colonial era. Outside the showers in American camps, I was still astonished to see posters saying "Iraqis not allowed." I fully understood that this segregation had arisen out of fear, but it nonetheless struck me as a sign of defeat.

When I got to FOB Speicher, another base in Tikrit, I asked to meet female soldiers who had reenlisted — I wanted to know why. Lieutenant Colonel Switlik introduced me to his best women soldiers, who he said could do everything men could do. There were eight of them in a semicircle, whites from Minnesota and blacks from Brooklyn, young single mothers and older women. Their reasons were always the same: they had all reenlisted for the signing bonus that would help support their families. They were all charming and intelligent, and each one cast a cold eye on the war they were engaged in.

I felt a great deal of sympathy for these women, who I found had a lively sense of humor. They were there, at great risk to their lives, to keep their families alive. They had not anticipated being trapped in this bizarre business. Nicole Paquin, a twenty-four-year-old blond blue-eyed sniper from Minnesota, told me that at first they had all just stared at one another, the whites from the country and the blacks from the city: "They looked at us like corn-fed shit kickers, and as far as we were concerned, we wanted to lock our doors when they went by." By now they had become lifelong friends, with a deep bond, as one experiences in wartime. "That friendship is the only thing we'll miss," said Paquin, "because other than that, not one of us really wants to be here."

Especially not Quez, a single mother of Colombian origin, who had come here only to secure a steady income and take care of her four-year-old daughter: "She doesn't know I'm doing this for her. When I left, she held on to me and cried. She hates the army." I commiserated. I had learned to repress the tears each time I left my daughter, showing only a joyful, positive face to her, reassuring her each time that I would soon be back.

Sergeant Escoffery, a magnificent woman from Jamaica, aged twenty-four, felt caught between her father, a bus driver in the National Guard who was opposed to the war, and her government. "It's weird. One country attacks us and we take revenge on another one. Who's responsible for the World Trade Center towers? Do I agree we should be here? No. Am I obliged to be here? Yes. I signed the paper. Besides, this is where the oil is, isn't it?"

Awilda Vasquez, aged twenty-five, from New Jersey, said: "We give candy to the children. We're not supposed to do it, but it's the least we can do for people we aim our weapons at. It's true that Iraqis don't treat their women well. And from what I've seen when I go outside the base, they live in mud huts. But what right do we have to think we're better than they are?"

"That's right," said Paquin, who didn't mince her words. "You have to understand the Iraqis. Imagine the scene: a guy comes to my place in a convoy, aims a gun at me, and shouts at me to get the hell out. I'd be really angry. I'm afraid we're in another Korea, stuck here forever."

From Tikrit, Stanley and I traveled to Baquba. I wanted to write about the army carrying out pacification operations there almost every day. Once again we were carrying our packs under a merciless sun. Ah, the life of war reporters! All the soldiers we came across were, like us, sweating profusely, but they were sipping Gatorade while we drank tepid water. Leaving our gear in a trailer set in the sand, we went straight to base headquarters. As on every Saturday morning, Colonel Salazar, commander of FOB Warhorse, would be giving a briefing about life on the base and bringing everyone up to date on operations in progress. At the end of the briefing came the prayer: "The Lord almighty, he is the king of glory." The chaplain then concluded by asking for a minute of silence for a soldier killed by an enemy bomb. Every Sunday, the amphitheater on the base hosted a variety of religious services. Although I never went to church, I did want very much to see one of these ceremonies. Religion was the sinew of this war, I now knew. At the service for the born-again Christians, the screen showed pictures of an ocean with words of sweet songs as background music. Everyone came up and spoke of his problems, how the Lord had helped him overcome them. There were many worries about debts and a few stories about drugs. Interestingly, the chaplain, Townie Pickens, an African American from Chicago, held an M-16 in one hand and a Bible in the other. "I was once a drug addict, far from God. But I tell you that God is more powerful than bombs. Here I am, with a new life. With Him, there's no accidental firing. Your M-16 won't help you in paradise. Here you have to think positively. Yesterday, I was on the verge of breaking. The heat was unbearable. There was no electricity. Thank you, God, I said. I'll never be hotter than I am today because I'm not going to hell."

I recalled what Hutson Niberley, a female soldier I'd met at FOB Speicher in Tikrit, had told me: "We don't understand why this war had to happen, but God has the keys. This war is a crusade, one religion against another religion. I was brought up in a Pentecostal church in Brooklyn and I remember the prophecy of the falling towers. Well, here we are." In this war, God had replaced the joints that used to circulate in Vietnam. I said to myself that these people were all really in good spirits. If I believed in God, I don't think I would have been grateful to Him for having thrown me into this mess and this scene of destruction, even for the sake of higher interests that I did not understand.

God, always God.

The next day, Stanley and I packed up again and left for FOB Gabe, far removed from Saddam's former palaces. It was a little camp of prefabricated buildings hidden behind sandbags in a burning desert. We were with one of the most prestigious infantry divisions in the American army, the famous Big Red One, known for having fought in World War I, and in World War II in the Normandy landings.

I especially liked this little base because it was on a human scale, like being on a college campus, with a tiny post office, an Internet café, a dining hall. I shared a trailer with the woman in charge of the mail, a young African American woman with two children, who relieved her boredom by listening to wonderful country music. She didn't understand why she'd been sent "urgently" to Iraq to take care of the mail in this burning desert. She had practically nothing to do. Had it not been for her country music, she would have gone crazy. Her days resembled those of a prisoner or a prison guard. She was the only woman I met at FOB Gabe. The camp held only men, professional soldiers. Congress had kept women out of ground combat forces because, as a discontented woman soldier had told me on another base, "American public opinion wouldn't have liked to see mothers come home in body bags."

Colonel Oscar Hall, commander of the 493 men on the base, knew every nook and cranny of "his" territory. He was a tall African American man with a baby face. I met him at lunch, where he described his methods. His warm, childlike laugh and candid speech made him seem like a character from a movie, funny and incredibly brave. He had survived five bomb attacks, a record. Because he had come away from all of them unharmed, he had concluded that he was invulnerable, a common syndrome in Iraq. "Here they understand the language of money and the language of power. And with my thirty combat tanks, I have what it takes," he told me. Hall participated in all the raids, every sortie "out there," into the hostile world beyond the concrete barriers of the camp, on which, painted in large white letters, were the words "FEAR GOD," the division's slogan. "During the invasion, there was a front line," he explained. "Here, as soon as you leave the base, it's like a western: things can come at you from anywhere. When we're on operations, I can hear all the clocks in my head — my helicopters, my Humvees, my men, the civilians I have to evacuate, the bad guys I'm after. I play all the parts. I'm the trainer, the mentor, the diplomat, the soldier, and the asshole."

I followed him uneasily as he strode through checkpoints and walked between police posts and Iraqi army positions. I counted at regular intervals: "Five, ten, twenty minutes, no explosion, nothing, still alive." Was he aware of the risks we were all taking? "They have to see our boots on the ground," he explained calmly as he walked beside the concrete barriers. After each dive "out there," I gratefully, and with some surprise, realized that we were still alive. "If I die, tell my wife that it was the colonel's fault," one soldier whispered to me, with a mixture of admiration and annoyance at his leader's daredevil courage. But to my surprise, the whole platoon escorting the colonel fought to maintain the adrenaline high of the Humvee patrol. "Hey, Jeff, do you have any room? I've heard things are cooking out there." After two days on the base, I'd become like them, looking for my danger fix and to get away from the desperate boredom of the camp.

Men in the division had been blown up by simple explosive devices, bombs stacked on one another, devices hidden in dead dogs or cows. The last one to have been hit was Dobson, a gentle captain with a round face who looked like Charlie Brown. "He was standing directly above the bomb that blew him into the air," Sergeant Major Ladisic said with awe. "He's everything you think." Without complaining, Dobson had come back to base barely two weeks before, after more than three months' hospitalization in the United States. He was still limping. "It was March second. Oh man, that date is more important than my birthday."

"It was especially the day when you cried like a little girl," joked the colonel.

For Sergeant Ladisic, his great day had been April 7. "I fainted. 'Sergeant! Sergeant!' My men were shaking me." The Humvee we were in still showed traces of shell fragments that had penetrated Sergeant Ladisic's right side. The door no longer closed completely, and it had been repaired countless times. Only the colonel traveled in an armored Humvee.

Some Humvees were jinxed, soldiers told me. When I got into the one they called the "bomb magnet," because it had been blown up five times in two months, like everyone else I put on a Jesus medallion without asking any questions. I touched it, not really believing in it, out of solidarity and mostly superstition. Several times a day I would jump into a vehicle going from one bomb attack to another, from a mass grave to a suspicious car. In fact, it seemed that most of our time was spent watching Iraqis gathering their dead. While I was in Baquba, the level of violence grew so intense that all the "cleanup" operations had to be canceled to deal with the immediate emergency. How in the world, I kept asking myself, did a nice girl like me end up volunteering in this nightmare?

One morning CNN reported the discovery of a mass grave containing twenty bodies in the desert between Baquba and Baghdad. The first thing we noticed when we got there was the overpowering smell. Since traveling in Iraq, I had trained myself to distinguish among corpse odors. There was the metallic fragrance of freshly shed blood, the headier smell of barely cold bodies, and finally the putrid stench, which made you nauseous and dizzy, of decomposing flesh. This stench, which lodged in my memory and still haunts my nightmares, was the one I smelled that day in the desert. A young sergeant next to me, overwhelmed like all of us, gave a comforting hug to one of his comrades as if to exorcise death. "If this isn't the stench of hell, then I don't know what is!"

The twenty bodies exhumed from this mass grave had already been sent to Baghdad for identification a few days before.

Only the horrible odor remained, trapped in the blood-drenched earth, in the scraps of entrails littering the ground, and the blankets that had been used to carry the bodies. We felt as though it would never leave our own lungs and clothes. I stumbled over skull fragments and jawbones. I offered to help the Iraqi policemen busily collecting them in plastic bags so I wouldn't have to stand there with my arms folded, strapped in my bulletproof vest under the burning sun. "It's just like an Easter egg hunt, you never know what you'll find," exclaimed Colonel Oscar Hall with his usual deadpan humor. The police chief told him that these people, who had been executed with a bullet to the head, were not from the province. Colonel Hall pointed out to the Iraqi that the mere fact he didn't know them didn't mean they weren't from here. "Iraqis don't reason clearly," he said. "I spend hours disentangling their convoluted logic." But the evidence was contradictory. On the ground plastic handcuffs had been found, something only American soldiers and the insurgents had. "Terrorists display the bodies of the people they execute, they don't try to hide them in the desert," said Hall, who finally guessed that this was a settling of scores between Sunnis and Shiites.

We had barely returned to the base when we learned that there was a firefight at a checkpoint. Not altogether recovered from the stench of corpses, I really wasn't ready for yet another expedition. Sergeant Major Ladisic gave his safety instructions as we piled into the Humvee riddled with shell holes. Everyone listened to him carefully each time he conveyed his orders. It was never a formality.

"Do what you've been trained to do."

"What if we're hit?" asked one soldier.

"I don't know, ask God."

Then Ladisic yelled to the gunner, "God damn it, hold your gun straight," and handed me a bag of gummy bears. The Humvee's gunner, his mouth full of candy, was constantly squatting down to protect himself when the danger was too great. As for me, I was in a state of numbness.

When we got to the spot, the first thing that struck me was the silence. Ladisic asked me where I wanted to start. I didn't know, I didn't want to start anywhere, but here I was, and there was no way out. I stared as though I were watching a movie. The ground was carpeted with bullets, blood was everywhere, and among the bullet-riddled bodies was that of a boy. The bodies of the police, most of them Shiites and Kurds, were unceremoniously dumped into a van. One arm stuck out; bodies were piled on one another, the dead so numerous there was no time to treat the remains with any respect. Once again it was clear that the Iraqi dead were not worth as much as "ours" — there were too many of them, cannon fodder. As a soldier named Patterson said to me, "I cry when I see Americans die. When my Iraqi friends die, I'm sorry, but they're not my people." So much for human compassion.

The place had to be cleaned up quickly to keep Iraqi morale from sinking even further. Policemen were sobbing, overwhelmed, worn out by all the violence. Others, nauseated by the spectacle, were vomiting off to the side. My head was hurting and I wanted to be somewhere else, but I hung on.

"Another marvelous day in Iraq," said the colonel. "Don't touch any body parts without your gloves."

"Jesus, it smells like death," said one of the soldiers, who looked green. "You wonder what you're gonna have for dinner tonight, don't you?" He asked me if I was all right, and I turned the question back to him. Puffing out his chest, embarrassed at having displayed his distress, even though it was perfectly understandable, he answered: "Me, I'm always fine."

"These towel heads didn't even have their bulletproof vests on," another one complained. The American soldiers wanted to fight against the enemy, be in the front lines instead of Iraqi soldiers and policemen.

"And if we're supposed to count on them for the security of the country," another one said, "then we're in this shit hole forever. These guys would screw up a wet dream."

I was surprised by the anger of the soldiers against the shat-

tered Iraqi policemen burying their dead. In the end, I understood their frustration. They really believed they would be more
effective against the enemy. It was true that the Iraqi forces had
not yet been adequately trained, and it was hard not to be exasperated with them when they neglected to put on lifesaving bulletproof vests. But it was not at all certain that American soldiers
would do any better at checkpoints or police stations. It was impossible to fight against an invisible enemy, and the Iraqis had
become scapegoats for the frustrated soldiers who dreamed only
of returning home.

We set out again, like long-suffering Sisyphus on his never-
ending labor, back in the Humvees in search of the enemy.
"These guys who kill their own children are religious termina-
tors," one soldier said, an apt description.

The colonel stopped a hearse — he had to be suspicious,
even of the dead. Sitting in another Humvee, I was amused by
the soldiers' mocking imitations of the colonel's voice and manner. They no longer believed in their leader's methods for stopping the insurgency. The endless violence had become an
obstacle course whose finish line had long ago been lost to view.
There was nothing left to do but to pat the Iraqi army captains
on the back as they buried their dead: "Sorry for your loss." And
so, life continued in this war zone.

The next day, a car bomb exploded in front of the police station in the little town of Kanaan. I saw, yet again, fragments of
flesh stuck on the windshield and the police station demolished.
Those who were still alive were attending funerals. Seven suspects,
all Sunnis, had been arrested and taken to Iraqi army headquarters for questioning. Abraham, an interpreter for the American
army, slipped into the tiny room where the prisoners were being
held. "We try to question them before the Iraqis do. When they
turn suspects over to us, they've grilled them so long and so hard
they can no longer talk, they sing!" he explained.

Were the Americans wincing at these methods? Had torture
been subcontracted, as some Iraqi officers had suggested to me? I
had no answers to these questions. They were a terrible flashback

to the debate on torture in Algeria that had resurfaced in France a few years earlier, when a French general had finally confessed his guilt and asked forgiveness from the victims he had tortured. I remember wondering at the time how human beings had been capable of committing such abominations. On a theoretical level, the practice outraged me as much as the death penalty. During the Algerian War, aside from humanistic scruples, the rational argument of those who denounced it was that it was useless, because torture victims would say anything and implicate anyone. I had felt so ashamed when the scandal of Abu Ghraib was revealed, ashamed of being a Westerner.

All during my many trips to Iraq, my outrage at torture remained constant, but I had gradually begun to understand how you could possibly come to that point. After the second time you see children blown to pieces in an attack, you are so outraged, you feel less concern about the way suspects are treated. The natural reflex is an-eye-for-an-eye. I understood the mechanism, even though I condemned the outcome. If U.S. soldiers thought that Iraqi officers could, by their "methods," prevent other Iraqi children from dying or could save their comrades from having their legs amputated, then they would close their eyes, if only to give themselves the feeling that they were doing something, dirtying their hands, not standing idly by as the butchery went on. After only a week of this tour through slaughter in Baquba, I fully understood the ordeal of soldiers who were impotent witnesses to the nightmare.

Later I watched the colonel, together with the Iraqi chief of police, counting the dead. "Be careful," he said, and "I'm sorry for your loss," the same words heard over and over again, meaningless, in the colonel's rather brusque tone, as though he were hurrying his sympathy along, eager to move on to something else. All of a sudden I heard him shout, addressing himself to the mayor of the town: "And you take it. You never give me any information about the bad guys." The mayor, who had already had a long day, started to cry. Nerves, and everyone's emotions, were raw. Everyone blamed everyone else for the attack; someone had to be found guilty for the unexplainable. A little down the road, another horror: a bomb had killed a little girl and two sheep. I looked at the animal carcasses, not very different from human carcasses, and all the pictures of bloody remains in dusty ditches blended together in my imagination: the filth in the hospital in Nasiriya, the contaminated garbage dumps in Basra. Horror pictures of a country that had been defiled.

The colonel held his men back: "Don't rush in. I'll assign someone. We don't all have to get blown up at once." I thought about the kids who came home with stumps or in wheelchairs, the ones who had become impotent, the ones who couldn't piss on their own. How long would their wives or fiancées still believe they had been heroes?

A session of "kicking down doors": houses in the area were being searched. I hated this. A watchdog bit a soldier's hand; another one took aim at the dog, hesitated, and finally refrained from shooting. I had noticed that American soldiers in Iraq were particularly sentimental about animals. They petted them, adopted them, gave them nicknames, as though their need for humanity had taken refuge in their relationships with animals. Shouts and dogs barking were everywhere, along with helicopters overhead.

My mobile phone rang. I answered instinctively, surprised I had a connection. It was my father from Paris, wanting to know how I was. "There are dogs with you? And what's that noise?"

"Yes, it's the base's dog. Don't worry, everything's fine." A pure but necessary lie.

In one of the houses, a man wearing a long white dishdasha had hidden two Kalashnikovs from the search. "Why did you lie to us?" yelled Abraham, the colonel's interpreter, a Christian from Baghdad. "He's a Sunni. I don't trust him, we have to test to see if he has traces of explosives on his hands." With an impassive smile, the man explained he had not understood what they had asked him. I wondered why he was so calm. It was almost as though he knew the modus operandi of the Americans, who had explained to me that excitement was always a sign of guilt. Colonel Hall returned the weapons to their owner and asked him for his help in keeping the road secure. He could have done the opposite, arrest him or have him tested. There were no rules, no method.

The next day, I went with Colonel Hall to the town hall of Khan Bani Sad. The mayor of the little town had asked to see him urgently. Naief al-Zaidi was one of the very few Sunni mayors in Diyala Province. A former high school physics teacher under Saddam, he had been mayor for two years. Wearing a light-colored suit, he greeted the colonel uneasily. Colonel Hall allowed me to sit in on the conversation in a corner of the mayor's office.

At first the two men and their translator, for reasons I couldn't fathom, were whispering, and I had to strain to hear the conversation. Then they grew heated and the volume rose with the tone. I was distressed. It was very clear and confirmed my worst fears. Their edifying dialogue was eloquent about what was happening in Iraq. Sectarian tensions were rising, and the inability of Americans to intervene, or more precisely their decision not to, posed the risk of seeing Iraqis slaughter one another.

"I asked to see you," explained the mayor, "because the situation is serious. Many people are complaining about the violence of Iraqi police and soldiers against prisoners. This violence is creating reactions that are snowballing. The coalition must help us."

"Why should we worry," answered Colonel Hall, "if the Interior Ministry arrests bad guys? That's the Iraqis' affair, it doesn't concern the coalition." Hall was intelligent and had to be aware of these problems. But I could see he was following orders like a good soldier.

"The Iraqi government is raising tension between Sunni and Shiite tribes. The Interior Ministry is all Shiites, and the Badr Brigade make unjustified raids on houses of Sunnis whether they're old friends of Saddam or not. And that's going on all over Iraq."

"Is that a fact or an opinion? Don't trust rumors. Remember

when they said that they were importing garbage from Iran to burn in the incinerator in Baquba."

"That has nothing to do with it. I'm talking to you about facts. Go and check the houses that have been searched and the lists of people arrested: a poor schoolteacher, an imam. The coalition questioned them, and the Interior Ministry arrested them again. This is serious."

"I can't do anything. An Iraqi judge will have to decide on their guilt. If they're innocent, they'll be released. Don't worry."

"Aren't you going to do anything to stop civil war in Iraq, sir?"

"If the chief of police wanted to start a civil war, he'd arrest all the Sunnis, including you, Mister Mayor. I don't understand your logic. Why don't you talk about the Shiites who died at the Muhammad Sacran checkpoint?"

"That's just it, the population now thinks the attack on the checkpoint was revenge of the Sunnis against the Shiites. We have to defuse the situation. My country is now governed by Shiites alone. They think Saddam favored Sunnis. That's false: if his own finger had risen up against him, Saddam would have cut it off. Saddam never made a distinction between Shiites and Sunnis. I know that Shiites say bad things about me, that I'm a terrorist, a Baathist. The Interior Ministry has a big file on me."

"You have never handed over a guilty person to me. According to you, the bad ones are always somewhere else. But you know that the boy who carried out the attack yesterday lived on the other side of the street? Don't bullshit me! The people who line up at your door are Sunnis, not Shiites." I wondered if the translator was conveying the change in tone and vocabulary, or whether he was softening the edges.

"They arrested thirty-five Sunnis in a little village. If they searched all the houses, it wouldn't be a problem. I don't want you to get angry. I want you to help us maintain stability."

"I'll ask you to be patient and wait for Iraqi justice to do its work. Don't spread rumors of civil war. If you stir up the flames, you'll get burned."

We left the mayor. Nothing had been resolved, as far as I could see. Conflicts would go on as before. And the civil war was already beginning here, spreading like wildfire in the districts of Baquba, the mixed city, eight months before the Samarra blast that forced diplomats and some soldiers to acknowledge the situation.

One night after dinner at FOB Warhorse, I visited the soldier named Patterson in his prefabricated hut, in such a state of disorder that his sergeant called it "little Fallujah." This twenty-one-year-old Californian was full of good humor, funny, a born actor. He mimicked his friends falling asleep during the March offensive. He read letters from his grandmother out loud for his comrades. He had become the local entertainer. He had tattooed his girlfriend's name on his arm, but she had left him since he'd been in Iraq. What he hated the most here were the insects. He made me laugh by acting out the long, the square, the huge ones with bizarre shapes that he found in his room, and showing me his body covered with bites. His description made me think of the fanatical sheikh in Fallujah speaking of the holy spiders who had come to help them against the American soldiers — maybe these insects were what he was talking about.

Patterson hated Iraq. "This country? I don't get it. Why do they hate us? Why are they mad at us when we got rid of their nasty dictator? Why do they keep on fighting? I don't have the slightest idea. For me, every Iraqi is a bad guy until he's proven innocent. If you drive toward us, I'll shoot you, and then afterward I'll have the time to be sorry. They kill. We kill. I feel good that I helped kill several dozen, that I saved American lives. Here, in two seconds, click, bang, you're dead. You have to look everywhere, listen to everything. And you don't know where to look," he explained, cleaning his weapon, an operation that took him thirty minutes every night.

"My .50-caliber Browning weighs thirty pounds. It's the greatest weapon, but it's a real pain. It can hit planes, trucks, so when you aim at a guy, he really gets it. One day I saw a guy who had nothing left but his skull; his whole face had been shot off, even his brain. If you're hit, pow, you explode."

At FOB Gabe, in the stifling night, I sat with some soldiers who'd taken off their uniforms and were playing cards, sipping Gatorade. Sergeant Mike Billings was talking with his friends, losing at poker. He liked his job when he was driving his colonel's tank at top speed down the road, the noise of metal, and the rattle of the machine gun. That morning Colonel Hall had taken Stanley and me on a tour in his tank, so I could understand the pride and pleasure he took in driving the impressive machine, his feeling of great power. We laughed as we sped by some astonished Iraqis. The colonel offered to let us shoot the machine gun. Stanley declined, telling the disappointed Hall that he shot only with his camera. I tried, out of curiosity and to please the colonel. The bullets had gone into the sand dunes around the camp. It felt like the video game soldiers were using to train the Iraqi army.

But Mike wanted to do something more useful in "real life." Despite the glittering promises the army held before soldiers to make them "sign the paper," despite the $10,000 bonus, he was not going to reenlist. He was thinking about going home. He didn't wear his combat medal, even though it was an honor he had richly deserved. "What good does that do? I know what I did. When I go home, I'll be a hero for some people, and a monster for others. But I'm neither one, just a soldier."

I would miss my soldier friends for a long time. For a while, I would feel bad for having deserted them. I had lived through a terrible but intense period. I even missed the base's lukewarm Gatorade and revolting salad bar.

I left Iraq without seeing Muhammad again, even though I wasn't far from his house, stuck waiting for my return flight in Camp Victory in Baghdad. But he didn't hold it against me. He knew that even though we were in the same city, our two worlds could not come together. He really wanted to come to see me, but the usually fearless Muhammad didn't insist. He acknowledged it was too dangerous. He was as afraid of car bombs as of being targeted by nervous American soldiers. I had never thought I would hear him say that — after all, he had come with me to interview al-Zarqawi's right-hand man in Fallujah. Two and a half years after the "liberation" of Iraq, the concrete walls erected between us in Baghdad had become impenetrable.

Epilogue

FOR THE past four years in Iraq I have been covering a war that belies its name. The devastating dual attack on the World Trade Center and the Pentagon was followed by a reprisal that was tragically misconceived. This truth becomes all the more real and relevant to me as I write this epilogue in Afghanistan, the abandoned battlefront. It was here that the response to 9/11 was supposed to take place, rooting out the Taliban and bringing peace to this long-beleaguered country. Yet five years after the attack on New York and Washington, the Afghan capital Kabul is a "green zone" in a country where the warlords have reasserted their hegemony. Barely two hours out of Kabul, I saw primary schools for girls burned to the ground by the Taliban, which clearly has not been eradicated. In my knapsack I have videos of propaganda made by Mullah Dadullah — the most wanted terrorist after Bin Laden — showing dozens of young recruits in the Konar Mountains, lining up to become kamikazes in exchange for a ticket to paradise. Following the example of the Iraqi jihadists, they too have carried out decapitations of prisoners and filmed them to boot.

In the media, the daily litany of the previous day's dead brings a glaze to people's eyes and minds, the numbers no more meaningful than those quoting the rise and fall of the world's stock prices.

As for me personally, when I'm away from the war, back home at my daughter's birthday party or with friends where I find myself laughing at their stories and anecdotes, I'm constantly beset by a series of relentless flashbacks of those I've seen killed, of those who granted me an interview and then, days or weeks later, were gone, murdered by one side or the other.

All these senseless dead.

Almost every day a taste, a smell, the image of a face, jolts me back to Iraq either momentarily or in a long, dark daydream.

But there are pleasant memories of Iraq too. I think of the complicit laughter I enjoyed with Salem's sisters, and of his mother's delicious cuisine. I also remember the endless discussions we had, which sometimes began at lunch and lasted until early evening, at the café al-Hiwar (The Dialogue), the last "libertarian" café in Baghdad, where the Iraqi painter Qasim Sabty blew kisses to the young ladies who were sipping their Turkish coffee, their heads uncovered even during Ramadan; the bitterness of the ice-cold pomegranate; the bits of pistachio shell in the ice cream at al-Faqma; Mazan's unerring sense of humor no matter what the circumstance; Adel's astonishing erudition. . . . Even in Baghdad, one could enjoy and savor moments of happiness.

Because the situation in Iraq degenerated so swiftly, worsening with each of my successive visits, I had the distinct feeling that the strategists were always at least one step behind, reacting to elements that were already altered. What, in my opinion, were some of the gravest errors? For one, invading a country where an aging dictator was already enfeebled and probably in the last throes of his reign, rather than focusing the available forces on al-Qaeda and attacking its bastions in the tribal regions of the Pakistani mountains. For another, trying to "de-Baathify" Iraq, emulating the de-Nazification of Germany after World War II, rather than trying early on to bring all sides together — Shiites, Baathists, Kurds — to form a true coalition government, which would also have had the positive effect of undermining and curbing the insurgents. Further, from what I observed, it was tactically wrong to give more and more power to the Shiites at the expense of the Sunnis even as the growing threat of civil war between the two factions was there for all to see. It seemed to me the Americans saw in Iraq — in the guise of Saddam Hussein or of al-Zarqawi — the incarnation of Absolute Evil, and thought that if only these devils were eliminated, all would be well. Shades of the Old West, where the constant focus of justice was on the Most Wanted list. Many of the Americans I saw and interviewed over those four years seemed surprised and upset when these Most Wanted leaders were killed or brought to justice and the Evil persisted, its roots seemingly spreading underground where it was hard, if not impossible, to find and eradicate them.

It was this glaring discrepancy between what I encountered and the description promulgated by the authorities and the official media that made not only me but other foreign correspondents on the ground often feel powerless, with a strong sense of the absurd. There were in fact times when I wondered whether my chosen vocation as a journalist would survive the Iraqi conflict.

Was I right to return to this stricken land time and time again? To take all these risks? Mind you, to be suddenly faced with danger, to find yourself in a life-threatening situation, is far different from reflecting upon it later, when doubt assails you. All I can say is, I still feel I did not entirely accomplish my mission. There are shadowy areas left to be probed, a curiosity not fully satisfied. For I still cannot fathom what goes on in the minds of the Fallujah torturers, any more than I can understand those who abused and tortured the Iraqi prisoners in Abu Ghraib or wantonly murdered in Haditha. Perhaps this explosion of barbarity on both sides transcends any psychological or political formula or process.

I do believe that if September 11 brought to light for the first time the vast chasm between civilizations, the war in Iraq brought to light a glaring example of the decline of the West. On the one hand, you had a democratic ideal so corrupted that it produced the prison at Guantanamo Bay, and on the other — perhaps in response — a violent nihilism of Muslim extremists. Two decadences confronting each other.

What have I learned about myself during these four years of covering the wars in Afghanistan and Iraq? I doubtless now have a better understanding of the contours of my courage and cowardice, even if those contours are in a state of constant flux. For instance, with each new visit to Iraq, I became increasingly concerned that I might not emerge alive, or at best come home maimed or wounded. In other words, I was more and more afraid of the consequences of each new foray into this land of hate. But I also understood, perhaps for the first time, what drew me back to these danger zones: today, when backpackers from every country crisscross the planet by the thousands, the areas of conflict like Iraq are the only path of adventure left — a no-man's-land where time and rules do not exist in the normal sense and where you are living your own novel each and every hour. I also know that my strength in these extreme conditions of violence and war emanates in large measure from the fact that I have a hard time dealing with the so-called normal aspects of life. The death of someone close to me, or an operation that my daughter has to undergo, is far more difficult for me to handle, and I realize that I am more courageous on the front lines of battle than I am in a hospital room. The vicarious suffering I have witnessed over the months and years in these deadly countries is no guarantee that I will be steeled against my own personal pain and suffering.

What's to become of Iraq? The fall and arrest of Saddam Hussein, and now al-Zarqawi's death, have given rise to various theories. As for al-Zarqawi, as someone who had intimate contact with his insurgent group, I frankly viewed his death as a nonevent. He was a symbolic celebrity, glorified both by being dubbed Bin Laden's second-in-command and by the Americans, who made far too much of him. The fact is, no sooner was he dead than he was replaced.

In Iraq, the present and future danger lies elsewhere, notably in the continuing threat posed by the guerrillas, who have brought the battle right into the streets of Baghdad. The possibility of civil war is real. Is the only solution to divide the country into three separate ethnic entities? That's the opinion of most of the pessimists with whom I have talked. Others, more optimistic, dream of a Mandela surfacing to save the country. I wish I could share their dream.

The American military has already announced the reduction of troops in Iraq starting in 2007. What will happen when the coalition troops depart? Obviously I can't say, but during my last visit, when I was with American soldiers in Baquba, I noted that nowadays they emerge from their bases less and less frequently to venture "out there," and when they do, it's usually to offer their condolences to Iraqi civilians whose families have been decimated by insurgents from one camp or the other. Despite the daily massacres that occur in that ethnically mixed city of the Sunni Triangle, one senses that the coalition forces consider it no longer their problem. The strategy of withdrawal is already well under way.

I know, too, that when the coalition forces finally do leave, the foreign correspondents will be swift to follow. How much longer will newspaper publishers and the reading public continue to read reports, in this world of sound bites and short memories, about that distant land?

I think especially of my Iraqi friends, prisoners in their own homes, who dream of the day when the explosions that rock their cities will cease, when the concrete barriers and barbed wire that interlace their streets will be gone and they will not emerge from their homes to stumble over viscera and body parts. If you sense I'm being overly dramatic, believe me, I'm not.

What am I left with? A plethora of contradictory thoughts. Guilt, as I write these lines, that I am not still in Iraq. I know that life must go on, but even in my moments of happiness, in the future I'll always carry with me the memory of the outrageous crimes to which I've been witness, always trying to understand how they are even possible.

More positively, I shall for the rest of my life try to remember, and apply, the many lessons in courage shown by those heroic men and women I met in Iraq.

Kabul, Afghanistan, June 2006